The Gospel vs. Torah

Conflicting theologies

Or the greatest love story never told.

The Gospel vs. Torah: Conflicting Theologies or the Greatest Love Story Never Told

Copyright © 2018 by James R. Pratt

Lexington, SC 29073

All rights reserved. This book or parts thereof may not be reproduced in any form, stored in any retrieval system, or transmitted in any form by any means-electronic, mechanical, photocopy, recording, or otherwise-without prior written permission of the publisher, except as provided by the United States of America copyright law. For permission requests, write to the publisher, at "Attention: Permissions Coordinator," at the address below.

Book Design by James Pratt

Cover by James Pratt

Edited by Brian E. Buffkin

First Printed Addition 2018

Faith Geniuses Enterprise

Heart Epochs

P.O. Box 6881 Columbia, SC 29203

Acknowledgements

The endeavor of writing this book could not have been possible without the grace, mercy, patience, and gentle leading of my King Y'shua. The love, support, and passionate excitement of my beautiful wife Alicia and my children Trinity, Isaiah, Hezekiah, Eliana, Shoshanah, and Evangelina pushed me through many times when I felt that I had taken on an impossible task. Finally, the constant encouragement of my parents (Jim & Karen Pratt), my brothers (Joshua & John Pratt), my pastor (Shane Richardson), and my entire church family at Heart Epochs were truly a source of strength and inspiration as I pursue the calling the Lord has given me. To Him be all the glory, and may everyone who came along beside me in this journey be blessed a hundred fold!

Table of

Contents

Chapter 1	IN THE BEGINNING...CHRIST	7
Chapter 2	GOD'S FRIEND	21
Chapter 3	A PEOPLE UNTO MYSELF	41
Chapter 4	WORTH FIGHTING FOR	52
Chapter 5	TRUST ME	69
Chapter 6	THE EGYPT IN OUR HEARTS	97
Chapter 7	PREPARE TO RECEIVE	122
Chapter 8	A GOD WE CAN TOUCH	138
Chapter 9	THE WARNING OF A FRIEND	177
Chapter 10	GREATER LOVE HATH NO MAN	196

Author's Note

When the Lord first called me to write this book, I could suddenly imagine how Noah must have felt when he was called to build the ark. Yet, when the Lord places something within you, you are consumed by the thought of it and you know that your only release will come through obedience. Like many believers, I was raised in a Christian home and grew up listening to many powerful teachers on TV and radio. After a while, I noticed that sermons seemed to become redundant. Pastors would focus on salvation, healing, or prosperity through the Word of God, and would often times take one scripture and build a ministry off of it. I soon found myself getting frustrated by it all, quickly losing my desire to even read the Word. I also found that many different denominations would speak against the doctrine of the other, and could back their views with scripture. So I began to ask myself how this was possible. How could Christ inspire 33 authors to write 66 books over the span of 1500 years and it be interpreted so many ways? What frustrated me the most was how all of these denominations could use the Word to back their beliefs and their interpretations would SEEM accurate. Then the Lord spoke something to me that I had never thought of before: the Bible was written by Jews, originally for Jews, about a Jew, and yet we know very little about the Jews and their culture.

Where did this incredible disconnect come from, this "anti-Semitic" approach to scripture? Was it caused by simply taking scripture out of context, or was it a plan of the enemy to remove the strong foundation of our faith? The title of this book was not just intended to be an eye catching phrase, but to address an age old-debate that has crippled our walk and understanding of the Word for years. As a result, we are left with half-truths and "revelations" that merely scratch the surface of the Word's true meaning. It is like simply watching the ending of an exciting movie, and then attempting to convey to people the story in its entirety. Or even worse: it's like getting married only for the intimacy without first establishing a relationship. This is what we have done by trying to create a "New Testament Church"; we have become so focused on the intimacy and blessing of God, that we have failed to solidify a foundational relationship in Him. In these turbulent times, and with the persecution of our faith ever increasing, simply playing church or using cute Christian catchphrases is not going to cut it anymore. We need to KNOW Him deeply. I have heard it said that God works in mysterious ways, to which I respond: "Only if you don't know Him." If you have a relationship with the Jesus Christ (or more accurately Y'shua), then you know His ways and there is no mystery in His faithfulness to us. For those who may not be familiar with the name Y'shua for Christ (rather than Yeshua), this translation comes from the One New Man Bible which I refer to throughout this book. I know it may seem a little different reading the name of Y'shua in place of Jesus, and I can assure you that the intent is intimacy. My first name is James, but my dad calls me Jimmy and my wife calls me "babe" or sweetheart." Though I answer to all of them, there is just something about it when my wife calls me "James." It makes the conversation so much more personal and it gets my heart going every time. Since this is a book on the Lord's heart towards us and His desire for intimacy; my hope is that by referring to Him in His Hebrew name, He would sense that same kind of love from me.

The goal of this book is to show that The Gospel and Torah are not conflicting theologies, nor is one used to "do away with" the other. The covenants are not done away with….they are built upon. John 1:1 says that "In the beginning was the Word, and the Word was with God, and the Word was God," and then later on in verse 14 John writes "And the Word became flesh and lived among us…." (One New Man Bible). This revelation that the Lord was giving to John regarding His Son was huge. Christ did not just know the Word, or live the Word, HE is the Word! Genesis 1:1 to Revelation 22:21 is the very DNA of who Y'shua is. He cannot deviate from or do away with the Word, just as He cannot deviate or do away with a part of His physical self. It is Who He is. So when the question is asked "Did Y'shua honor Torah or did He fulfill it while He was on the Earth," the answer should be "Yes!" Christ both honored Torah and fulfilled its true meaning, giving a level of understanding to his disciples that baffled the "experts" and religious leaders of their time. It was this kind of Biblical understanding that made fishermen and tax collectors the pillars of our faith today. Even more incredible is the commission that the Lord gave his disciples in Luke 24:44-48 (Verse numbers may be different in other translations), "And He said to them [the disciples], These are the messages I told you while I was still with you, that it is necessary for everything that has been written about Me in the Torah (Teaching) of Moses and in the Prophets and the Psalms. **Then He opened their minds and they understood The Scriptures**: and He said to them that thus it has been written that the Messiah would suffer and be raised from that dead on the third day, and repentance would be preached in His name for forgiveness of sins for all the heathens. Beginning from Jerusalem you are witnesses of these things" (One New Man Bible, Bold added for emphasis).

In the "Great Commission," the disciples are commanded to go into all the Word and make disciples of all men. So here, Christ has opened the minds of His disciples to the fact that He was the reason He ordained HIS feast, the animal sacrifices, the Ark of the Covenant, the alters, and so many other commandments that may not have made much sense at the time; but when now viewed through the lens of Himself, the disciples realize that all of these things had been declaring Y'shua from the beginning!

So what happened between then and now? How could the minds that were once opened to scripture suddenly be struggling for revelation? The answer is the doctrine that parts of the scriptures that were foundational for the writing of the "New Testament" have been "done away with." This is being taught even though Y'shua clearly says in Matthew 5:7-8, "Do not think that I came to do away with, or to bring an incorrect interpretation to, the Torah or the Prophets: I did not come to do away with but to bring spiritual abundance, for the Torah (Teaching) to be obeyed as it should be and God's promises to receive fulfillment. For truly I say to you: until the sky and the Earth pass away, not one yod (smallest letter in the Hebrew alphabet) or one vav (second smallest letter in the Hebrew alphabet) could ever pass away from the Torah (Teaching), until everything would come to pass." Without this foundation, we are left grasping for straws with regards to the life of Christ and the words that He spoke. As my friend and former pastor used to say "we need to circumcise our Bible." What he meant by that was we needed to tear out that one blank piece of paper that separates the Old and New Testaments in our Bibles, and come to the realization that the two books are actually one. My heart is that as you read this book, you will come to the same two revelations that the Lord has given me: 1) You are not loved...you are adored beyond what you can comprehend, and 2) that the Lord is absolutely and completely in control of ALL things. There is a love and sovereignty to our God that has been hidden from us by the design of our enemy Satan for centuries. But praises be to our God who said "In the last days I will pour out My Spirit upon all flesh!" With the out pouring of His spirit comes the revelation of who He is, and a deeper understanding of His love for us that can sustain our faith not matter what the future may hold. You know who Jesus is; now, let me introduce you to Y'shua Meshia - Our Saving Messiah!

Chapter 1

<u>In the Beginning...Christ</u>

You may not know this, but the Torah (The first five books of the Bible) is broken up into what is known as "Torah portions" which were (and still are among the Jewish and Messianic believers) required reading every Shabbat or Sabbath. The first of which in our Bibles is Genesis or "B'reshite;" loosely translated to mean "Beginning," a deeper understanding of this word "at the head of" or "Creator." Even more incredible, the first letter in the Hebrew language is "Alef" which (believe it or not) is not spoken and represents God. The second letter of the Hebrew Alphabet is the letter "Bet," which represents Christ and is the first *spoken* word! To take it even a step further, during John's time the term "Logos" or "word" was used to try and describe a "supernatural consciousness," that was believed by the Greeks to have created all things. This "consciousness" was believed to be so incredibly powerful that its full power was beyond any understanding.

This makes John's revelation so profound in John 1:1 and 1:14 when he said that "In the beginning was the Word (Logos/Bet) and the Word was with God, and the Word was God...And the Word became flesh and lived among us, and we saw His glory, glory in the same manner as the only child of the Father" (One New Man Bible or ONMB). So here Christ is using John to completely confound minds of both the Jews and Greeks by telling them the first spoken word, the one that is at the head of all things, that incredible and indescribable force that was beyond comprehension: that was Y'shua whom you crucified. Both the language that He gave the Jewish people and the once pagan belief of the Greeks were both declaring who Christ was from the very start. What an introduction for Yehovah (Hebrew name for God) to give for His Son, one that must have floored those who first heard it. This is first example of many of how the Lord was setting the stage for what was to come. As this very familiar passage in Genesis continues, the Lord gives us a step-by-step process of how He created all of existence. The wording and description is so simple, yet what was accomplished is baffling scientist to this today.

There is a powerful glimpse of God's heart hidden right before our eyes in Genesis 1:3-5, that I have read over for years. It says, "And God said Light Be! And there was light. And God saw the light, that is was good, and God divided the light and the darkness. And God called the light Day, and the darkness He called Night. And there was evening and there was morning, day one" (ONMB). In all of the times that I have read this passage, I have just assumed it to mean that the Lord created the day and night as we know it today. Yet, you'll notice that the sun and the moon are not created until Genesis 1:14-15. "And

God said, Lights, Be in the Firmaments of the heavens, to divide the day from the night! Be for signs and for appointed times (which is Mo'ed in the Hebrew, it also means Feasts) and for the days and years! Lights, Be in the Firmaments of the heavens to give light upon the earth!" So here we have two separate sources of light, the first being Christ Himself and the second being from the sun. I believe that the first light that Christ created was to reveal to creation the knowledge of who He is. You see this theme carried throughout scripture of darkness being ignorance of Christ, and the light being the knowledge of Him. An example of this can be seen in both Isaiah 9:1-2, and then repeated in Matthew 4:15-16. "Land of Zebulun and of Naphtali, way of the lake, beyond the Jordan, Galilee of the heathens, the people who dwell in darkness saw a great light, and to those who dwell in the land and darkness of death a light rose for them" (One New Man Bible). What an incredible thought that one of the first things Christ created was the ability for us to know Him!

Another example of this was well-covered by Joe Amaral in his book "Understanding Jesus." Joe shows a link between the Feast of Tabernacle (or Booths) and Christ being the Light. In 2 Chronicles 7:1-3 we read, "Now when Solomon had made an end of praying, the fire came down from heaven and consumed the burnt offering and the sacrifices and the Glory of the Lord filled the House. And the priest could not enter the House of the Lord, because the Glory of the Lord had filled the Lord's House. And when all the children of Israel saw how the fire came down and saw the Glory of the Lord upon the House, they bowed themselves with their faces to the ground upon the pavement and worshipped and praised the Lord saying, For He is good! For His loving kindness endures forever!" What is happening here is Solomon is dedicating the Temple (or House of the Lord) during the feast of Sukkot or Tabernacles. We know this because of 2 Chronicles 5:3 reads, "Therefore all the men of Israel assembled themselves to the king at the feast which was in the seventh month." Solomon finishes dedicating the Temple and the Lord Himself moves into a manmade structure! The creator of the entire Universe is content with living in something His creation built. It would be like your child building a house out of cardboard, and you leaving your five-bedroom lake house to live in it, just so you could be near them and they could be near to you.

Since that incredible event, the eighth day of the Feast of Tabernacle has become known as the "greatest" day of the Feast according to John 7:37. Later on in John 8:12, on this same "greatest" day, Y'shua makes the connection for those who would listen. It says, "So Y'shua spoke to them saying, I AM the Light of the world: the one who follows Me could **not** walk in darkness, but will have the light of life." Christ just declared to the children of Israel that He was the same Light that filled the Temple; on the same day that the event took place many years before! I love how the Lord always reveals Himself in a way that we will know it was Him. Y'shua's heart is to be known by us, to declare to us all that He has done for us, and to prove that He has been there with us all along. Y'shua then goes on to embody this same light in us when he said, "Your light must now shine like this before all mankind, so that they would see your good deeds and they would glorify your Father, the One in the heavens." We carry in us the Light that was created on the first day, the Light that filled the Temple, the Light of Life, and are called to fill the earth with that Light!

A relationship broken:

So the Lord has created the ability for Himself to be known, but what use is it without someone to give it to? This brings us another amazing insight into the heart of God: His overwhelming desire to have a relationship with man. In Genesis 1:26 we read, "Then God said, We will make mankind in our image, after our likeness and have dominion over the fish of the sea, over the fowl of the air, over the cattle, over the earth, and over every creeping thing that creeps upon the earth." What better complement can you give a new dad then to say that his son looks just like him? Y'shua didn't just haphazardly create man; He made him in a way that all of creation would know who he belonged to and came from. Can you imagine being Adam when he opened his eyes for the first time? The first thing he sees is the adoring face of his creator saying, "You are good, you are so good, and you are mine." To take it even a step further, the very next thing the Lord does is show Adam everything that he created for him and Eve! What a breath-taking gift to give your children: the Lord wasn't satisfied with letting them be part of His creation; He wanted them to have it. And to show that His relationship with them didn't stop there, He commanded them to conquer the world that He created knowing that they would need Him to do it. "And God blessed them and said to them, Be fruitful! Multiply! Fill the earth! Subdue it and have dominion over the fish of the sea and over the fowl of the air and over every living thing that moves upon the earth!" (Genesis 1:28) Has the Lord ever called you to do something that was so far beyond you (like writing a book while helping raise six children and having a full time career), that you knew immediately that you could not do it without Him? Have you ever stop and asked yourself if maybe that was His plan the whole time? In order to develop a deep relationship with Christ, we often times have to be put into situations where we have to trust Him on a whole new level. Sometimes that requires tremendous sacrifice, but we'll get to that later.

    A true relationship must be tested; the option to reject Christ must be present in order for our love for Him to be genuine. As we know, Adam and Eve are given that option in the form of the tree of knowledge of good and evil. How amazing is it that the first lie the enemy tempted man with was the thought that the Lord was keeping something from them? To this day, all sin that we struggle with is based in that very same lie. To be fearful or anxious is to believe that the Lord is withholding His goodness or faithfulness from us. To steal or covet is to believe that God is withholding provision from us. To struggle with drugs, alcohol, or pornography is to believe that the Lord is withholding His comfort, His joy, and His healing from us. He declares in His word, "Then what will we say pertaining to these things? If God is for us, who can be against us? He in fact did not spare His Own Son but gave Him over on behalf of us all, then how will He not freely give us all things with Him?" (Romans 8:31-32) Yet, just as we do so often, Adam and Eve traded everything they had for the one thing they did not. It is not the fall that jumps out at me in this portion of scripture, but how the Lord of the entire universe responded.

    In Genesis 3:8-9 we read, "And they heard the **voice of the Lord God walking** (the Word of God walking...Christ) in the garden in the cool of the day, and Adam and his wife hid themselves from the presence of the Lord among the trees of the garden. And the Lord God called to Adam and said to Him, Where are you?" (Bold and emphasis added) Have you ever wondered why the Lord asked Adam where he was? There is nothing hidden from the Lord and He knows all things, so I believe another insight to God's heart is hiding here in plain sight. He wasn't asking where Adam was physically; the Lord was asking were their relationship went. I can almost hear the Lord saying, "Didn't we walk together in the cool of the day and talk? Did we not name the animals together and speak face to face? What happened to us?" The Lord could sense in His heart that something had been lost, that a relationship He cherished above all His creation had been broken. But even then, the Lord didn't kill them, torture them, or leave them to fend for themselves. Instead, He clothed them, told what they needed to do to feed themselves, and continued to be with them even though the relationship had been severed. We know this because later on in Genesis 4, the Lord speaks with Cain regarding his offering. This is such a powerful truth about who Christ is and His heart towards us. In Hebrews 13:5b we read the promise that, "For He said, I will not abandon you and I will not ever forsake you." Here in Genesis, we see this characteristic of God being lived out. Adam and Eve had just sentenced Christ to death with one act of disobedience; yet God still saw His image in them, and He knew that there was something in them worth fighting for.

    Just like our Heavenly Father, we have within us the desire and the ability to fight for what we love. Yet our advisory, the Devil, will try to convince us that the battle is already lost. To which we can declare, my King of Kings did not stop battling for me, so I will never stop fighting the good fight of faith! Not in my walk, not in my marriage, or with my children! The battle belongs to the Lord and through him, I have the victory!

God's Love Language

There is probably not a testimony in the Word (events that actually happened aren't referred to as stories) more epic and more controversial then the life of Noah. I have spoken with devoted Christians who still have a hard time stating with confidence that the flood actually took place. Despite the debate and the evidence on both sides, to dismiss this historical event is to miss out on a characteristic of God that flows though the Word. In Genesis 6:5-8 we read, "And God saw that the wickedness of man was great in the earth, and every imagination of the thoughts of his heart was continually only bad. And the Lord was sorry that He had made man on the earth, and it grieved Him in His heart. And the Lord said, I shall destroy man, whom I have created, from the face of the earth: man, beast, the creeping thing, and the fowls of the air, for I am sorry that I have made them. **But Noah found favor in the eyes of the Lord.**" At this point in history, man and the world alike were consumed in wickedness. The Bible even goes so far as to say that there were giants in the land and that these "leaders" (also translated elohim, powerful men, of false gods) were "knowing" the daughters of men (Genesis 6:4). Even with this absolute perversion of all that God had created, you'll notice that His response was not anger-but grief. The Lord could have just as easily destroyed all that had been created and started over, but Noah's faithfulness had caused him to find favor with the

Lord. What an incredible thought that in the midst of all of the evil that consumed the world, the endless sin could not distract God from the simple, daily acts of faithfulness that Noah lived out every day. The Lord commands Noah to build an ark (the word for ark in Hebrew is Tevah which means "box" and is the same word used to describe Moses' basket) and Noah was obedient. That right there is, in my opinion, the "Love Language" of God.

There a wonderful book by Gary D. Chapman called The Five Love Languages, in which you can discover the five most common ways that we show and receive love. After reading this book, which helped my marriage tremendously (by the way), I began asking myself "What is God's love language?" Sure, we tithe, go to church, worship, and even help the poor and less fortunate; and all of these things are right and fruits of our salvation. Yet, I still felt that there was something deeper that really stirred the heart of our God, and I believe He revealed it to me through His Word and prayer. God's love language is obedience. Y'shua cements this truth in John 14:21, "The one who has My commandments and keeps them, that is the one who loves ME: and the one who loves Me will be loved by My Father, and I shall love him and reveal Myself to him." At first, this may seem rather simple or even common sense to an extent; but if you really stop and meditate on this point, it screams of the importance of relationship. If we don't obey God, it's because we don't trust Him. If we don't trust Him, it's because we don't know Him. If don't know Him, then how can we say that we truly love Him?

If a stranger were to run up to you as you walked out of the mall and said, "I need $500, it's an emergency!" We would probably respond one of two ways; we would either hand him a $5 dollar bill and wish him luck, or we would tell him we didn't have any cash on us and we would call the police as soon as we could. However, if a close family member were to knock on your door and make the same plea, we more than likely wouldn't hesitate. Why? Because of the relationship we have with that family member that was developed over time. We know them by their character and past acts of love, that if they are asking for money, then they must truly need it. To live in the world the Bible describes during this time, Noah would have had to have seen the faithfulness of God time and again. The Bible speaks of giants, demons, and mankind who have completely given themselves over to their evil desires. And yet, we find Noah and his family alive and unharmed; moreover, the Lord was faithful enough to keep three women from the demon's grasp so Noah's sons could have wives. Noah didn't have a church or Bible studies to attend. He didn't volunteer in kids' ministry or go to Wednesday night services. All he could do is be faithful and committed to the God that he was introduced to by his father; a God whom had been passed down for more than a thousand years. Noah's heart of obedience caught the eye of God amid all of the chaos He was ready to destroy. This brings us to the next glimpse into God's heart, and that is the fact that He is more concerned about faithfulness than numbers. The relationship that the Lord had lost with Adam He found in Noah, and He was willing to go to extreme lengths to show Himself faithful as a result. We see this same desire for faithfulness in John 6:53, which says, "The Y'shua said to them, Most certainly I say to you, unless you would eat the flesh of the Son of Man and you would drink His Blood, you do not have life in yourselves." Later in verse 66 we read, "For this reason many of His disciples left for the things behind them and they were no longer walking with Him." Earlier in this same chapter we find that the same large crowd that Y'shua had fed before was with Him again.

    This time the crowd came seeking a sign and wanted to be fed by a miracle again. Instead of appealing to the crowd and starting His own "Mega Church," Y'shua throws them a curve ball they were not expecting. In a statement that to the undiscerning listener would sound like a horrible violation of Torah, Y'shua tells them to eat His flesh and drink His blood. The Lord wasn't after the crowd's allegiance; He was after their hearts and would rather have twelve faithful than thousands of lukewarm followers. Even after the multitudes left, Y'shua tested the hearts of His disciples and I loved Peter's response. Starting in verse 67 we read, "Then Y'shua said to the twelve, Now do you want to go? And Simon Peter answered Him, Lord, to whom will we go? You have the words of eternal life, and we have believed and we have known that You are the Holy One of God." In a nut shell, "Lord, I don't get, but I trust you." The Lord could have easily destroyed all of mankind with one angel and Noah could have simply watched the reward of the wicked. But the Lord wanted to test the hearts of His faithful by asking them to do something that was far beyond them. He wanted them to demonstrate their love for Him in a way He received it most, through an act of total obedience. As a result, eight lives were spared out of billions, and God's undying desire to have a relationship with His creation continued.

Chapter 2

God's Friend

I am sure you can tell by the title of this chapter where our next glimpse at God's heart is leading us. The relationship between Abraham (or Avraham in the Hebrew) and the Lord is one of the most incredible loves stories in the Bible. What an amazing thought that a God who could be spending His time exploring the ends of the galaxies that He created; watching stars be born and walking the face of planets we couldn't hope to reach, would rather spend His energy with one faithful heart. Long before Pentecost, the woman at the well, or even blind eyes being opened, there was a simple man who grew up in a world full of gods. Then the Lord did something that none of Abram's false gods could do...He spoke to him and made Himself real. The Lord commands Abram to leave all that was familiar and go to a land that He would show him. Notice that the Lord didn't tell Abram where he was going, but he was quick to listen and he took Sarai and Lot with him. As I've said in the chapter before, I believe that the Lord's love language is obedience, which may be why (knowing Abram's heart) He chose Abram to be the founder of our faith. The boldness of Abram's faith was evident right from the beginning as well. In Genesis 12:5 we read "And Abram took Sarai his wife and Lot his brother's son and all their possessions that they had gathered, and the souls that they had made in Haran: and they left to go into the land of Canaan, and they came into the land of Canaan." The portion of this scripture that reads "and the souls that they had made" are disciples that began to follow Abram's preaching. Its one thing to tell people that a statue will bring them protection or luck, but it is quite another to look someone in the eye and tell them that you have spoken audibly with the creator of the universe. I love the pattern that the Lord is continuing to use as we go through His word. Once again the world has fallen into sin, but this time under the leading of Nimrod (Genesis 10:8), who along with his wife Samuramous, had created the belief known as the "Mysteries" as well as Astrology. This belief system had turned the whole world on its head spiritually, and the world was once again quickly heading back to its "pre-flood" state. Yet, instead of being filled with rage at mankind ruining its second chance at existence; the Lord decides once again to use one man to change the course of history.

  Later in Genesis 12, Abram is faced with his first real test, which he fails miserably. Abram was fearful that because Sarai was so beautiful, the Egyptians would kill him to have her. So Abram asks Sarai to pretend to be his sister so that he could live and she agrees to do so. Thanks a lot, Abram…love you too. As Abram predicted, the Egyptians saw Sarai and brought her before Pharaoh with the understanding that she was not married. Pharaoh even pays Abram with livestock in exchange for her, and

Abram accepts it! Here is where another part of God's character comes into play, how He is faithful to defend His plan in our lives. Jeremiah 29:11 tells us that "He knows the plans that He has for us..."and He will never falter in that plan. Instead of leaving poor Sarai to suffer due to Abram's fear, the Lord sticks to the plan He has and delivers them.

In Genesis 12:17-20 we read, "And the Lord plagued Pharaoh and his house with great plagues because of Sarai, Abram's wife. And Pharaoh called Abram and said, 'What is this that you have done to me? Why did you not tell me that she was your wife? Why did you say, She is my sister? So that I took her to be my wife. Now therefore behold your wife, take her and go your way.' And Pharaoh commanded his men concerning him. And they sent him away, and his wife, and all that he had." How great is our God? Not only does He deliver Abram and Sarai from Pharaoh, but He has Pharaoh send Abram away with the livestock that Pharaoh had given him for Sarai. When we are willing to be obedient to the Lord in His leading, we do not have to fear failure. He is faithful to deliver us even from our own poor decisions, fears, and best intentions. I love how the Lord swings for the fences in His demonstration of faithfulness towards Abram. No different than a guy wanting that first dinner date to be perfect, or the girl spending hours getting ready so she could look "just right" for him. I believe the Lord was setting the bar high for Himself in the eyes of Abram. He wanted Abram to know that He was able to do "beyond measure far more than we ask or we imagine according to the power which works in us for our benefit." (Ephesians 3:20). There is another powerful pattern here that we will see later on in the Torah. Here is a hint: plagues coming upon Egypt due to a bride being held unlawfully, and then the bride being sent out with gifts. Sound familiar? The Lord is even gracious enough to warn Abram that it was coming, despite the fact that it would take place long after Abram was gone. In Genesis 15:13-16 we read, "And He said to Abram, Know of a surety that your seed will be a stranger in a land that is not theirs and will serve them and they will afflict them four hundred years. And so that **I AM** will judge the nation whom they will serve, and afterwards they will come out with great possessions. And you will go to your fathers in peace: you will be buried in a good old age. But in the fourth generation they will return here again, for the iniquity of the Amorite is not yet full."

      To take it even further, this bride that is being held and persecuted is a perfect representation of the Christian church today; and I believe that is how the Lord views us as well. Sure, there is a plan and a purpose for our lives while we are here on the earth; but have you ever wondered why the Lord would refer to his church as His bride? I can't help but see the similarities, and it fills my heart with joy to know that He is returning for the righteous with the passion and excitement of a groom on his wedding day.

His Faithfulness in spite of us

Having saved Lot from four armies with only three hundred and eighteen men, and the Lord cutting a covenant with Abram promising him all the lands of his enemies, Abram finds himself still aching for the greatest desire of his heart. Only this time, Sarai has taken notice of the Lord's "slow" response to their prayers. Interestingly enough, this is the first time that we see Sarai provide Abram with her opinion of what the Lord is doing. As so many of us do, we get fearful that the Lord is going to miss the "proper timing" (or, if we're honest, "our timing") of when a miracle needs to occur. So Sarai gives Abram Hagar to be his wife and she conceives a son named Ishmael. In case you were wondering where all of this chaos involving ISIS and "Radical Islam" is coming from, just look at the Lord's prophesy of Abram's first born son. In Genesis 16:11-12 we read, "And the angel of the Lord said to her (Hagar), Behold, you are with child and will bear a son, and will call his name Ishmael because the Lord has heard your affliction. And Ishmael will be a wild man. His hand will be against every man and every man's hand against him, and he will dwell in the presence of his brothers." Even in all this mess, you still see the commitment the Lord has to the promise that He made to Abram. Back in Genesis 15:5, the Lord tells Abram that his decedents would be a numerous as the stars. The spoken word of God has creative power, and the Lord spoke to Abram that his seed would produce nations. This promise, being fulfilled in a son that should have never been, again shows the faithfulness of our God to his Word. Abram was 86 years old when his "plan B" took place; and once again, the Lord's response was not the rage of the "Old Testament God" that we have been taught. The Lord appears to Abram when he is 99 years old and declares to him that "I AM the Almighty God! (El-Shaddai)" In Genesis 17:5, we see the Lord do something that I didn't fully understand until recently, the changing of Abram's name. The text reads, "Neither shall your name any more be called Avram, but your name shall be Avraham; for I have made you a father of many nations." Another name for the Lord is YHVH, and though the name "Yehovah" comes to mind, the true meaning goes so much deeper.

     YHVH in the Hebrew is "Yod Hey Vav Hey" and it has been said that this name symbolizes the breath of God. Even more incredible, it is also to symbolize our breath in that every time we breathe in and out, we are declaring His name! The "H" in the "Hey" is strongly pronounced and is similar to the eighth letter in the Hebrew alphabet "Chet." The Lord placed His breath of life in us, and as a result, we declare His name day and night! What does this have to do with Abraham? The "H" in Abraham's name is strongly pronounced as well, suggesting that the Lord placed Himself or His breath into Abraham's name. The Lord was so committed to His promise to Abraham that He not only placed His spirit in Abraham, but in his name as well. What a personal touch for such a powerful God to place in one man's life. How would we pray if we knew that our Heavenly Father "Yod Hey Vav Hey" desires that same level of intimacy with us? Again, this is long before Pentecost and all of the well-known loving miracles that Christ did in the New Testament. So many pastors are teaching, whether they know it or not, that the Lord really didn't truly start caring about us until Y'shua was born. Yet, here we see a level of intimacy was not repeated until Peter, and is spoken about in scripture well into the book of Hebrews. When we think of God's love, our minds have a tendency to go to the scene of Y'shua asking Peter if he "agaped" Him ("Agape" being the Greek word for an unconditional love); but, how many of you have heard of the Hebrew word "Hesed?"

According to William Morford (author of the One New Man Bible that I have been referencing) "Hesed is a Hebrew word that defies translation. Hesed is love, mercy, favor, grace, forgiveness, kindness, gentleness, patience, and more rolled into one." If there is no shadow of change in our God, then it should be no surprise that this level of love would be throughout scripture. When you see any of one these listed characteristics of God in the Old Testament, then "Hesed" is what the scripture is referring to. Selah (which means "pause and think on that").

This next part I have heard debated time and again as to who the individual was that came to Abraham; but as we look through the scripture and have already seen the Lord's heart toward Abraham, it is not too far of a stretch to identify his visitor. Starting in Genesis 18:1-4 we read, "And the Lord appeared to him in the plains of Mamre and was sitting in the tent door in the heat of the day. And he lifted up his eyes and looked, and there were three men standing by him. And when he saw them, he ran from the tent door to meet them and he bowed toward the ground and said, 'My Lord, if now I have found favor in Your sight, do not pass by, I pray You, from Your servant: let a little water, I pray you be brought to wash your feet and rest yourselves under the tree." Notice what is said here: the Lord appeared to Abraham and he looks up and sees three men. Then, when he is speaking with one of them he calls him "My Lord," and every reference to this person is capitalized. Most people agree that this was the Lord and two of His angels, but I like asking the question "Who is the only physical manifestation of God that we know of in scripture?" What is the answer? Christ! It is the voice that Adam and Eve heard "walking" in the garden! Abraham is talking face to face with the King of Kings and Lord of Lords, and is being allowed to serve Him.

As we read further on, we find that the Lord's plan was to go to Sodom and Gomorrah to destroy them. However, the Lord (or in this case Christ) knows that a friend of His (Abraham) has family there, and He doesn't want to hurt someone His friend loves. This should be so encouraging to us that our God would even think this way; but that is the kind of love and relationship that He had with Abraham, and He wants to have the same with us. Also we see that the Lord wanted to let Abraham know face to face that the fulfillment of His promise to him was at hand. It is almost as if the Lord is saying, "I knew how much this would mean to you, so I wasn't going to reveal it through an angel or some vision. I wanted to look you in the eyes and tell you that I have not forgotten what I promised you." Even Sarah receives encouragement after she laughs at the Lord promising that they will have a son this time next year. Instead of anger at her unbelief, the Lord simply asked her in verse 14 "Is there anything too hard for the Lord?"

    To reaffirm the point that the Lord considered Abraham before judging Sodom and Gomorrah, it is as if we are allowed to hear what the Lord is thinking in verses 17-19. "And the Lord said, Will I hide from Abraham that thing which I am about to do, seeing that Abraham will surely become a great and mighty nation and all of the nations of earth will be blessed in him? For I know him, that he will command his children and his household after him and they will keep the Way of the Lord, to do acts of loving kindness (Hesed) and judgment, so the Lord may bring upon Abraham that which He has spoken of him." Could there possibly be a greater desire of our hearts than to have the Lord say that "He knows us?" The Lord then says that He knows Abraham will raise his family to keep the Way of the Lord. This is the first time in scripture that the term "the Way" is used; and it seems to me that this is not only referring to the commandments of God, but that Abraham will encourage his family to seek the same level of intimacy with the Lord that he had.

Come, let us reason

When I think about all of the times that I have argued with God, I quickly remember that I have not won any of these disputes. However, when I think about the few times I have reasoned with the Lord, I began to ask myself why I don't do it more often. Now when I say "reason," I don't mean trying to talk God out of something, but rather asking for an insight into what He is doing so as to strengthen my own faith. Yet in Genesis 18:23-32, we see what looks like Abraham on the brink of arguing with God. Abraham knows that the Lord is on His way to destroy two cities and all who inhabit it; and for Abraham, this is a side of the God he has never seen before. Abraham has seen God's Hesed time and again, but now he was witnessing first hand a righteous Judge. In verse 25 we read, "Far be it from You to do after this manner, to slay the righteous with the wicked and that the righteous should be like the wicked: far be that from you. Will not the judge of the earth do right?" Even though the wording here seems extremely forward; almost as if Abraham had forgotten his place, but it also tells of the kind of relationship that he had with the Lord. This wasn't him defying his God, but rather pleading with a friend to change their mind. Still the Lord demonstrates His love for Abraham by allowing (yes allowing) Himself to be "reasoned" down to sparing the cities, if He could find ten faithful in them. I am convinced that the Lord knew what

He was going to find in Sodom and Gomorrah; the Bible even tells us in verse 20 that "...the cry of Sodom and Gomorrah is great and because their sin is very grievous." So the sins of these two evil cities have been crying out to the Lord for some time; which begs the question: why didn't He simply tell Abraham that instead of going through the trouble of being "bargained" with? I think the answer is twofold: first being that the Lord wanted to show Abraham He could be trusted in His judgments. Abraham seemed to believe that the Lord was acting to hastily in His desire to destroy these two cities, and was asking God to consider other alternatives. By allowing Himself to be reasoned down to ten men, the Lord brought Abraham to a place where he could reach the same conclusion that He Himself had already come to. The Lord knew their hearts and He wanted Abraham to see it as well.

    What benefit is it to our faith and growth for the Lord to do something, and we not be allowed to come to a place of maturity to understand why He did it? A crucial part of being able to trust someone is coming to know how they think and their reasonings. If you have a working knowledge of that person's heart; even if what they do doesn't make sense at the time, you will always assume it is for your good. Secondly, I believe the Lord had this conversation with Abraham to once again show the love that He had for him. The Lord doesn't have to justify His actions to His creation; like I have often told my children when they don't understand why I am asking them to do something: I say "Because I said so." This very easily could have been the Lord's response, but He did not want to hide His ways from His friend. Again, this is how trust is established.

The Lord once again shows Himself faithful too in the way that He delivers Lot from the punishment of Sodom and Gomorrah. When Abraham gave Lot the choice of where he wanted to go, Lot chose Sodom knowing the kind of city that it was. In Genesis 19:8, Lot offers his virgin daughters to the mob that was trying to get to the angels, so they could "do to them as is good in their eyes." This leads me to believe that Abraham's walk did not have much of a lasting impression on Lot. Yet when he first saw the angels coming in Genesis 19:1, he recognized who/what they were and he bowed himself down to them. How merciful is our God that he would give Lot (who is not walking with the Lord) such discernment to house the two angels who would end up saving him and his family's lives? However, it is what is written in Genesis 19:29 that makes this entire event so powerful for me: "And it was, when God destroyed the cities of the plain that **God remembered Abraham** and sent Lot out of the midst of the overthrow, when He overthrew the cities in which Lot dwelled." (Emphasis added) This tells me one thing: God didn't save Lot for Lot, but rather, God saved Lot on behalf of His friend. If you are praying for salvation of a family member, a friend, or your own child, this passage should stir your heart! God is not only going to save them for their sake, but because He remembers you and He looks for opportunities to demonstrate His love for you. Even when they make bad decisions and bring hardships upon themselves, or surround themselves with the worst kind of company, our God is faithful to deliver them!

Tested Love

    I believe one of the greatest ties between the Gospel and Torah is the testing of Abraham's faith through Isaac. So far, the Lord has shown Himself faithful to Abraham time and again. He even appeared to Abraham face to face to tell him that Isaac's birth was near. Now suddenly out of nowhere, the Lord commands Abraham to sacrifice what he loved so dear. As I read the story of Abraham, I see what I have come to call the "Three phases of a spiritual battle." The first phase is when we are asked to do something, or faced with a challenge that seems far beyond what we can possibly handle. It seems as if we spend more of this phase simply trying to regain our footing before we can even take the first step towards trusting the Lord. I can only imagine that this command took the wind right out of Abraham. As we read the account in Genesis 21, we find that the journey for Abraham and Isaac took three days (or three phases). The second phase is the mental battle we face during the trial. This can be the most challenging and most important part to all spiritual warfare. If you lose heart and you allow fear, doubt, and unbelief to take hold of your thoughts, then defeat is almost guaranteed. I can say from personal experience that I have forfeited battles to the enemy, simply because I allowed myself to focus on the difficulty of my circumstances instead of the greatness of my God.

I can see Abraham and Isaac sitting around the campfire the second night of their journey talking; and Isaac asking "Father? Tell me about my birth again. Tell how the Lord came to you and said that Mom would have me even though she was older. Tell me about how the Lord told you that I would become a mighty nation," each word pulling at Abraham's heart and testing the deepest reaches of his faith in God's plan. Phase three is the day or time when the rubber meets the road, either the Lord will come through or all will be lost. Though this can be the scariest time of all, it is also the time when the strength and wonder working power is fully manifested. On day three, Abraham finds himself at the foot of Mount Moriah where the Lord has commanded him to take Isaac.

We pick up the account in Genesis 21:5-8, "And Abraham said to his young men, You stay here with the donkey and I and the lad will go yonder and worship, and come again to you. And Abraham took the wood of the burnt offering and laid it upon Isaac his son, and he took the fire in his hand and a knife, and they went up both of them together. And Isaac spoke to Abraham his father and said, 'My Father.' and he said, 'Here I am my son.' And he said, 'Here are the fire and the wood, but where is the lamb for the burnt offering?' And Abraham said, 'My Son, God will see to it, providing a lamb for a burnt offering for Himself.' so they went, both of them together." There is just so much here in these passages that just scream Christ and the type of faith that Abraham had. First, we see Abraham tell his servants that he and Isaac were leaving to worship and they would return again. Abraham makes this statement of faith knowing that he is about to go kill his son; and yet, the wording here speaks of both of them returning from worshiping. Fast forward to Hebrews 11:19 and we read that, "...so he (Abraham) considered then that God was able to raise Isaac from the dead, from which then, figuratively speaking, he took him." Other translations say that Abraham "reasoned in his heart..." that God was able to raise Isaac from the dead. This again is a level of trust that could only come through time and God showing Abraham continued acts of faithfulness. Abraham trusted God to His word, even though he believed for something that had never happened before. As we walk closely with the Lord, we will come to a place where we aren't concerned if the Lord has done it before, but we can simply rest in the knowledge that He is able.

Next we see the portion of scripture where it says that Abraham "took the wood for the burnt offering and laid it upon his son Isaac." When I read this, I see the figure of Christ being represented in Isaac, in that the wood that was going to be used for his sacrifice was placed upon him, just as the wooden cross of crucifixion was placed upon Y'shua. Then, they both carry the wood of their sacrifice up the same mountain! It is a common belief that Mount Moriah later became known as Galgotha where the crucifixion of Christ took place. One of the reasons for this belief was found by William Morford when he wrote, "Moriah, meaning 'Yah (God) is the Teacher,' speaks of the future Jerusalem, the seat of the Jewish teachings." Ever wonder why the Lord led Abraham to this specific mountain? If there anything that I have learned in my ever-growing study of the Hebrew culture and language, it is that the Lord never does anything without a purpose. There is nothing random with our God! Finally, we see that Abraham makes the statement that "God will see to it, providing a lamb for a burnt offering for Himself." The Amplified Bible uses the wording that the Lord will provide a "perfect sacrifice" for Himself. I believe this is Abraham prophesying about the Lord providing Y'shua as a sacrifice for us all. The Lord Himself tells King Abimelech that Abraham is a prophet in Genesis 20:7 and uses the Hebrew word for prophet "Navi." As we read on, we find that Abraham bound Isaac and laid him on the altar. As I have read this scripture so many times before, I have always assumed (and have been taught) that Isaac was a child about 12-13 years old when this happened. However, there are many studies (including one in the ONMB by William Morford) that state that Isaac was 37 years old at this time! That would have made Abraham approximately 137 years old; and chances are if Isaac wasn't a **willing sacrifice**, there would have been nothing that Abraham could have done to make Isaac get on that altar. This is yet another foreshadowing of Christ in the gospels; no one took His life, He laid it down willingly. Just as Abraham is about to slay his son, the Lord stops him and makes a somewhat confusing statement that could be one of the greatest insights into the Lord's heart.

In Genesis 22:11 we read, "Then the angel of the Lord called to him out of heaven and said, 'Abraham, Abraham!' And he said, 'Here I am.' And He said, **Do not lay a hand on the lad! Do not do anything to him!** For now I know that you revere God, seeing that you have not withheld your son, your only son from Me." You notice that the term "the angel of the Lord" was the one who stopped Abraham from killing Isaac. In the Amplified Bible (and other translations as well), the word "angel" is capitalized whenever this term is used. That is because it is believed that "The Angel of the Lord" was referring to Christ! Now, I am not implying that Y'shua is an angel; many scriptures throughout the Word declare that He is the Son of God. However, I believe that those who saw a pre-incarnate Christ knew He was more than just a mere angel, but they did not have a name to reference Him by. You'll notice in scripture that after Christ is born this term is never used again. You'll also notice that the "Angel of the Lord" in this passage tells Abraham that "For now I know that you revere God, seeing that you have not withheld your son from **Me**." Nowhere is this passage does "the Angel of the Lord" stop talking and the Lord starts. What I found so insightful about this passage, in reference to the Lord's heart, is where the "Angel of the Lord" (or Christ) says "For **now** I know that you revere God." The

Amplified uses my favorite wording when it says, "For now I know that you **love** God." The wording here suggest that the Lord learned something from Abraham's actions that He did not know before; which is a striking contradiction to our understanding that God is "all knowing." So why would the Lord use this wording when He was talking to Abraham? Then I asked myself the question, "Does the Lord have human emotions?" If we are created in His image and He is the One Who placed them in us, then is it too far of a stretch to say the Lord feels just like we do?

Time and again we see in scripture where the Lord grieved, was angered, Hesed, and has been referred to as a "jealous God." So I wonder if the Lord was testing Abraham to see the depth of the relationship He could trust him with, and how much of His Heart He could give Abraham access to. It's almost as if the Lord is saying, "I want to trust you with everything I have to offer, but I have been hurt before. I once walked with man side by side not withholding any part of Myself from him, but he still chose another over Me. I need to know that you have not replaced Me as well with Isaac." I know this seems like a radical thought, especially when we are raised in the church believing that, besides the fact that He loves us, we serve a stoic God. I know that when we think of our emotions, we think of how quickly they can be used to cause us to sin. But what would perfect love; infinite mercy, fullness of joy, a tender heart, and righteous anger look like? From the Bible I read, it sounds like the description of our God who is able to experience all of these without sin. We serve a God that desires to be pursued, that fights for our hearts, and that ever lives to intercede on our behalf.

How many times have we prayed from a standpoint that we had try and convince God to listen; or even worse, that we had to somehow earn the right for Him to bless us? We are adored by majesty, and that never changing love has been from the beginning. We have to change our view of God from this distant, all powerful being that is more than able (but is just complaisant) to a supernatural being that is both fully consumed and committed to an intimate relationship with us. I love how God sent "The Angel of the Lord" (Christ) to stay Abraham's hand; Y'shua wasn't about to let Isaac endure a death that was His to bear from the foundation of the world. This whole scene was the perfect display of what was to take place with our Heavenly Father and Y'shua. I believe the Lord was both testing Abraham's heart, and placing an earmark in history that we could look back on and know the heart of our God was the same even in Torah.

Chapter 3

A People unto Myself

Our next step in this journey to discover God's heart leads to a dynamic shift in the kind of relationship He is seeking. Up to this point, the Lord has been using and developing relationships with individuals (Adam, Noah, Abraham and Job, if you are reading the Word in chronological order). Now, we see the Lord wanting a nation set apart for Himself in the form of Israel. In his faithfulness to individuals, we see certain kings and kingdoms being blessed, but now the Lord desired that the whole world see how good He truly is. However, before we go any further, I would like to point out yet another unique and powerful pattern that the Lord has been using to show His heart. In Genesis 16:1-2, we find that Sari has bore Abram no children and Sari even says, "…the Lord has restrained me from bearing." In Genesis 25:21, Isaac "entreated the Lord for his wife (Rebeccah), because she was barren." And in Genesis 29:31, Jacob's wife is suffering from the same fate: "And when the Lord saw that Leah was loved less, He opened her womb, But Rachel was barren." Sarah was Abraham's wife when the Lord called him. Rebeccah was very specifically chosen by God (Genesis 24), and Jacob worked 14 years for Rachel (Genesis 29), whom the Lord would later bless. So the question here is why does the Lord keep choosing barren women for His chosen men to wed? So many times it seems like God's plan doesn't make any sense, and often times it is because we can't see where **we** get the glory in it. The only problem with that view is: in the end, it's not about us. The Lord will always do things in a way that brings Him the most glory. He used barren women to show that this was a lineage He Himself was establishing.

From His protection to His salvation, we see this desire of God's heart carried throughout scripture. How many times have we heard it taught: "Not by might, nor by power, but by My Spirit says the Lord (Zechariah 4:6)," or "For you have been saved grace through faith. And this is not from yourselves, it is a gift from God: it is not from works, so that **not anyone could boast**." (Ephesians 2:8-9, Emphasis added) Y'shua even drove this point home with His disciple when they questioned Him about a blind man. In John 9:1-3, Y'shua's disciples were asking about a man blind from birth, and whether it was because of the man's sins or the sins of his parents. In verse 3, Y'shua answered them, saying, "Neither he nor his parents sinned, but so that the works of God would be revealed in him." I remember hearing Pastor and Author John Piper say one time (and I am paraphrasing), that the most selfish thing God can do is not declare His greatness to us. I can see how the Lord may appear arrogant and self-absorbed in the way He describes Himself. However, when the Lord glorifies Himself, men are drawn to Him and they are exposed to His incredible love, mercy, and faithfulness.

When a man is glorified, we are then drawn to someone who will fail us and leave us empty. So as we continue to reveal that Y'shua's heart in the New Testament has been God's heart all along, I hope this insight will help explain His sometimes "strange" way of doing things…not only in scripture, but in our everyday lives.

    Now we come to Jacob the "heel catcher." Even from his birth, he has wanted all of the blessings of the first born and was willing to deceive to get it. From convincing his brother Esau to sell his birthright for a bowl of soup, to going to extreme lengths to trick his father Isaac into giving him the blessings of the first born, it is hard to imagine that the Lord would use this habitual liar to become Israel. We pick up the account in Genesis 32 where Jacob is about to see Esau again for the first time in twenty years. As I said before: Jacob took Esau's birthright, his blessings, his authority over his people, and Jacob is not expecting the warmest of welcomes. In fact, Jacob in convinced that Esau is going to kill him and his family. In Genesis 32:10, we see that it was the Lord who commanded Jacob to "return to your country and to your kindred." Remember what I said earlier about God's plan not making sense sometimes? Here is a great example of that and how the Lord Himself is glorified. Jacob is so sure of his fate, that he divides his house hold so that if one group was killed the others can flee. Yet before they reach Esau, Y'shua reinforces His promise to Jacob face to face! Jacob comes across a Man (notice the capital M in Genesis 32:25) who wrestled with him until morning. Even though the Man told Jacob to let Him go, he would not until the Man blessed him. In Genesis 32:28-29 we read, "And the Man said to him, 'What is your name?' And he said, 'Jacob.' And He said, "Your name will no longer be called Jacob, but Israel, for as a prince you have power with God and with men, and you have prevailed."

As I have said before, there's only one physical manifestation of God that we know of and that is Y'shua. This shown in verse 31 where we read, "And Jacob called the name of the place Peniel, for I have seen **God face to face** and my life is preserved (emphasis added)." Also, the Hebrew word for "man" is "Ish" which can be translated as "Husband," and Christ is our Bridegroom. I love how Christ asked Jacob what his name was; again, asking a question to which He already knows the answer. It's as if Christ is asking, "Tell me where your faith is in my promise to make you a nation, so I can take it to the next level." So before Jacob faces his greatest fear, the Christ changes his name from Yaakov (Jacob, "Follow Close After") to Israel (Prevailing with God). The encounter comes with a price and Israel is left with a limp; which (interestingly enough) would prevent Israel from being able to flee and save himself when he was in sight of Esau. He is now in a place that if Esau doesn't kill him, only God could get all of the glory.

In Genesis 33, Jacob sees Esau coming with four hundred men and it looks as if his worst fears were correct. There is no turning back now. Jacob sends two hundred she-goats, twenty male goats, two hundred ewes, twenty rams, thirty nursing camels with their colts, forty cows, ten bulls, twenty she-donkeys, ten foals (per Genesis 32:15-16), and sends them ahead of them as gifts to appease Esau. In Genesis 33:4, we see the heart of the "New Testament God" on display in the Torah. The passage reads, "And Esau ran to meet him, and embraced him and fell on his neck and kissed him, and they wept." Sound familiar? Try the parable of the prodigal son! Verse 10 reads "...for now that I have seen your face, **as though I had seen the face of God**, and you were pleased with me." This entire section of scripture has the picture of us and God all over it. How many times have we turned from God, and taken His gifts and talents and used them for our own gain? Maybe you are running from God right now because you believe that He will be like the Esau Jacob feared. I can promise you with all certainty that you will find the same unexpected, overwhelming response of love that Jacob found. Can you see the beautiful parallel that the Lord is creating here? Yet many times we try to be like Jacob and appease God with acts of righteousness, church attendance, or "Christian lingo." When all the while, He wants to just run to us, fall on our necks, and kiss us.

  The Lord takes the picture of His love a step further than the one painted in the prodigal son. Notice how in Genesis 32:18-21, Jacob is commanding his servants to take the herds of livestock he is offering to Esau and walk in front of him. That means when Esau saw Jacob coming and ran to embrace him, **he ran past all of the offerings!**

Giving tithes and offerings is a great thing and commanded by God to do; but we miss His heart when we try to <u>earn</u> His favor or blessings through giving. I believe that the Lord is grateful for generous hearts, but it is us He is after and He will run past our offering to get to us. Even when we are covered in the filth and shame of our sin like the prodigal son was; even if we have rejected His love time and again, His heart is screaming "Please! Come home and let me love you!" His Hesed is new every morning and His arms stretch from everlasting to everlasting. Notice that Esau could have run up to Jacob and said, "How dare you show your face around here? You took everything from me, and now here you are and I am supposed to forgive you?! You have done far too much to warrant my forgiveness." But he didn't, and when you come back to the Lord with a heart of repentance, you will **never** hear Him say that either…I promise.

Not Abandoned

      We now come to the historical account of Joseph and how God used the ruler of the known world to preserve His people. As I've said before: this concept of God showing himself faithful to a nation is still a new one at this point; this faithfulness would soon be put to an incredible test. Just like with Jacob, Joseph is shown a promise from God before he has to endure a hardship. In

Genesis 37:5-11, the Lord shows Joseph his future authority in dreams of his brother's wheat bowing down to his, and the Sun, Moon, and stars paying homage to him as well. I find it interesting that Joseph would later be able to interpret dreams accurately, but he could not discern the meaning of his own. The dreams and lack of discernment will play a power role as we go along. Another amazing little "teaser" that God put into this story is the "coat of many colors." According to William Morford, the phrase "many colors" is not in the Hebrew, but is found in the Greek Septuagint and the Vulgate (Latin). The literal translation here is "long tunic" which was similar to a poncho, and is believed to be the first "prayer shawl" because it went wrist to wrist. The prayer shawl played an important role in the ministry of Y'shua and would help to declare who He was. This was also a symbol of authority which is why Joseph's brothers hated him even more when they saw it.

 As we know, Joseph's brothers sold him into slavery to Ishmaelites for twenty pieces of silver. Joseph betrayed by his own and handed over to his enemies for money: sound familiar? Just as the Lord did not abandon Christ when he was betrayed, we see this same level of commitment towards Joseph. As we continue to read, we find that Joseph is sold to Potiphar and made a house slave. Even then, the favor of the Lord was upon him and Potiphar gave him charge over his entire house hold except his wife. As you know, Potiphar's wife is attracted to Joseph and tries to seduce him. Joseph is now faced with one of the greatest tests that a man of God can face: "Do I trade the vision for temporary gratification?" Joseph has already been given two dreams showing him in a place of powerful authority, so he knows that something great is on the horizon.

However, he also knows that his life at the moment is pretty good and Potiphar's wife was more than likely very beautiful. As I read this passage, my mind immediately goes to another scripture with a very similar temptation: the temptation of Christ in the wilderness. Matthew 4 records the event of Christ being in the wilderness for forty days, and being physically weak and hungry. Of the three temptations that was thrown at Y'shua, the one I see relating back to Joseph is where Satan takes Christ to the top of a mountain. Matthew 4:8-9 reads, "Again the devil took Him to an exceedingly high mountain and showed Him all the Kingdoms of the world and their glory and said to Him, 'I shall give all these things to You, if after You fall on your knees You would pay homage to me." The Lord already knew that these kingdoms would be His, but he also knew the price He would have to pay to obtain them. The enemy was offering it to Him for free, and all he would have to do is simply bow down and worship him. No stripes, no nails, no cross, just a simple act and everything He was going to die for would be His.

I can see the enemy lying to Joseph in a very similar way, "You know the dreams you had of being worshiped?

This is it! And to top it all off, you have a beautiful woman that wants to be with you. She must recognize the power and authority you have." I wonder how many men of God now could pass this test and hold onto the promise. Joseph resists the relentless temptation of Potiphar's wife and is accused by her of rape. Potiphar, through an act that could only have been God's mercy, sends Joseph to jail rather than kill him immediately. While in prison, Joseph again is given tremendous favor and is soon running the jail. I remember T.D. Jakes saying one time in a sermon, "Anyone can be a prince in a palace, but how many of you can be a prince in prison?" Joseph is then asked to interpret the dreams of two fellow prisoners; in Genesis 40:8, Joseph tells them that the interpretations come from God and asks them what they dreamed. What a tremendous transformation this hardship has brought about in Joseph. He went from being a spoiled brat who lied about his brothers and didn't know what his dreams meant, to being a man of God even in prison with the ability to give words of knowledge. Joseph interprets the dreams correctly and is then forgotten about for two more years!

    Then, in the Lord's ever perfect timing, Pharaoh just happens to have a dream and the cupbearer just happens to remember Joseph. Joseph is then brought before Pharaoh, gives glory to God for discernment, and tells Pharaoh of the famine that is about to come upon Egypt. Pharaoh places Joseph over all of Egypt and due to the famine, Joseph's brothers are forced to come to Egypt to buy food. This is where Joseph's visions come full circle. Genesis 42:8-9a says, "And Joseph knew his brothers, but they did not recognize them. And Joseph remembered the dreams which he dreamed of them…" Joseph's brothers are there for food, and amazingly enough, the dream that Joseph had of his brothers bowing to him was symbolized by their bundles of wheat. As I mentioned before: I find it interesting that Joseph could interpret dreams, but not his own. The revelation was hidden until the timing was right, and we see Y'shua use this same tactic when He was developing a relationship with His Disciples.

From demonstrating His power, to His transfiguration on the mountain, God revealed portions of Himself to them at the times when it would matter most. Today, the Lord continues to reveal Himself to us at times when it will have the greatest impact in our lives. The most important thing is to not miss those times, especially when they appear hidden in hardships. When Joseph finally lets his brothers in on the secret of who he is, his eyes are completely open to what the Lord was up to all along. In Genesis 45:4-7 we read, "And Joseph said to his brothers, 'Come near to me please.' And they came near. And he said, 'I am Joseph your brother, whom you sold into Egypt. So now do not be grieved or angry with yourselves that you sold me here, for God sent me before you to preserve life. The famine has been in the land for these two years, and there are still five years in which there will be neither plowing nor harvest. And God sent me before you to preserve you for a heritage in the earth and to save your lives by a great deliverance. So now it was not you who sent me here, **but God**. (Emphasis added)" Our King will not always reveal His plans for us; but rest assured if the Lord has promised you something, He can even use your enemies to bring it to pass.

Chapter 4

Worth Fighting For

    I would be lying if I said that I haven't been chomping at the bit in expectation of getting to Exodus! There is so much of the Lord's heart on display as He fights for the love of His chosen people. Yep, you read correctly: God is fighting for the love of His people. A people that have spent over 400 years in a nation that did not fear the God of Abraham, Isaac, and Jacob; instead, they worshiped gods of gold and stone made by man. Moreover, Israel has seen these idol worshipers prosper while their God appears silent as generation after generation suffer. A Pharaoh had come to power who did not know Joseph and who feared the number of the Israelites. This fulfills the warning that the Lord gave Abraham back in Genesis 15:13-16 when He said, "Know of a surety that your seed will be a stranger in a land that is not theirs and will serve them and they will afflict them four hundred years. And also that I Am will judge that nation whom they will serve, and afterward they will come out with great possessions. And you will go to your fathers in peace: you will be buried in a good old age. But in the fourth generation they will return here again, for the iniquity of the Amorite is not yet full."

The fourth generation spoken of here is counting from Isaac being the first, and the fourth being the generation after Joseph. To counter the ever growing number of Israelites, Pharaoh ordered that all male children be thrown into the river. Even now, early on, we see a parallel to Christ in that the enemy attempts to thwart God's plan by trying to kill His chosen deliverer while He was still a child. In order to save Moses from this horrible fate, the Bible says that his mother made a "box" for him out of bulrushes, slim, and pitch. The word "box" here in the Hebrew is "Tevah" and is the same word used for Noah's ark! Not to mention according to William Morford, the word for "pitch" in both cases is better translated as "Atonement." God's chosen deliverer is laid in a basket sealed by Atonement. Moses is then discovered by Pharaoh's daughter and allowed to be nursed by his biological mother.

When Moses was fully grown, he went to see the oppression of the Israelites and he saw an Egyptian striking a Hebrew. Believing that no one was looking, he killed the Egyptian and hid his body in the sand. This random act begs the question, "What was Moses thinking?!" He lived in the house of Pharaoh and was raised as a son of the most powerful ruler on earth. Why would he risk it all for one Hebrew slave? After all, this would not have been the first time that Moses saw a Hebrew being beaten. You remember the parable of the talents in Matthew 25 and Luke 19? In that example, the Lord uses money that brings back a return on the investment to symbolize what the Lord is looking for when He returns. I believe those talents also represent our callings. The Lord has placed in us His spirit and His power, and He wants a return on that investment. What's even more incredible is that the Lord will call forth that which He has placed within us, sometimes when we least expect it. If you don't believe me, just ask Paul. We see this playing out in Moses' unexplainable decision to act. The Lord had placed in Moses a call to protect and deliver his people, long before the burning bush even made him aware of it. The next day, Moses' actions are called out when he tries to prevent two Israelites from fighting. Knowing that word would soon reach Pharaoh, Moses runs for his life into the wilderness and eventually ends up in Midian.

      Moses lives in Midian forty years, gets married, and has a son; however, the bondage of Israel was still at the fore front of the Lord's heart. This is where we find the first glimpse into the Lord's heart towards Israel in Egypt. In Exodus 2:23-25 we read, "And it was over a process of time that the king of Egypt died, and the children of Israel sighed by reason of the bondage and they cried and their cry came up to God by reason of the bondage. And God heard their groaning, and God remembered his covenant with Abraham, with Isaac, and with Jacob. And God looked upon the children of Israel and God knew about them." In a very powerful study, Pastor Mark Biltz of El Shadiah

Ministries taught about the "13 Attributes of God;" and gives tremendous light on God's heart in this passage. One of the attributes that Pastor Biltz teaches on is "Chanan," which is Hebrew for "gracious" even to the undeserving. This word also denotes grace, beauty, charm, and loveliness. In this passage, God sees, hears, and knows the suffering of Israel. Pastor Biltz spoke on this saying, "Seeing is understanding the circumstances, hearing is taking it to heart, and knowing is having a personal knowledge though experience about what is to happen." The Lord isn't just somewhere far off watching His people suffer; He is neck deep in it and He is not going to allow Moses to abandon that calling He has placed within him. Hebrews 4:15-16 says that, "For we do not have a High Priest Who is unable to understand and sympathize and have a shared feeling with our weaknesses and infirmities and liability to the assaults of temptation, but One Who has been tempted in every respect as we are, yet without sinning. Let us then fearlessly and confidently and boldly draw near the throne of grace [the throne of God's unmerited favor to us sinners], that we may receive mercy [for our failures] and find grace to help in good time for every need [appropriate help and well-times help, coming just when we need it]. (Amplified Bible)"

_I Am_

The time for Moses to be idle in what most would consider a "normal life" has come to an end. As he tended to his father-in-law's herd on the far side of the mountain, Moses has an encounter with God that would turn his whole world upside down. In Exodus 3:2 we read, "And the angel of the Lord appears to him in a flame of fire out of the midst of a burning bush and he looked and, behold, the bush burned with fire, yet the bush was not consumed." Notice again that the Bible says "The angel of the Lord," which we have established with Abraham was Christ. Yet, there is another title that Y'shua reveals about Himself in verse 6. "Moreover He said, "**I Am** the God of your fathers, the God of Abraham, the God of Isaac, and the God of Jacob." This powerful revelation is twofold in this passage with regards to Who He is and His heart towards us. First, the Lord describes Himself as the God of Abraham, Isaac, and Jacob. What a humble title for a limitless God to take on. He measures the universe by the span of His hand, the Sun can from His lips in spoken word, He formed all of the countless stars in Heaven and knows them by name. And yet, He is content in simply being called the God of three men who harkened to His voice. Y'shua was trying to bring His awesome power and authority down to a level that Moses could understand. Awe-inspiring, but approachable. All-consuming, but desiring to be loved. Not a God of unrestrained wrath and judgment, but one who seeks a close relationship with us.

The second revelation in this passage is the "I Am" or "Anokhi" (One New Man Bible) in the Hebrew. While speaking with Moses, Y'shua does use the wording "Ehyeh Asher Ehyeh" or "I will be as I will be" declaring that there is no change or end to His power. But what I love about Anokhi is that it translates as "Because I Am." Y'shua is telling Moses to proclaim to Israel not that their deliverer is coming, but that their **deliverance** is coming! This blew my mind because it changed everything that I thought about the Lord's ways. It's not what He does, it's who He is! He is not just our healer, He is our healing. He not just our provider, He is our provision. He is not just our Savior, He is our salvation! This means that we don't have to guess whether or not God will do something, He is all that we need. Y'shua calmed the storm in Matthew 8:23-27; but in Matthew 14:22-33 He walks out to meet them and lets the storm rage. When the disciples begin to fear believing that He is a ghost, He tells them in verse 27 "…You must be courageous! I Am! Stop being afraid!" During the first storm, Y'shua showed that He could bring calm to the wind and waves. During the second storm, Y'shua declared that He is the calm in the storm! In John 11:24-25, Miriam and Martha are weeping over the death of their brother Lazarus, and Y'shua tells her that her brother will rise again. "Martha said to Him, 'I know that he will rise on the last Day in the resurrection.' Y'shua said to her, '**I Am** the Resurrection and the Life: the one who believes in Me, even if he would die, he will live." Our faith is stirred and our prayers are strengthened when we realize that to have Christ, is to literally have all that we need.

    As we continue on with this incredible conversation between God and Moses, Moses quickly realizes that what the Lord is asking is far beyond what he is capable of doing on his own. Moses is afraid that the children of Israel will not believe him; and the Lord gives him three signs for the people in the form of his staff turning into a snake, his hand being covered and cured of leprously instantly, and pouring river water onto dry land and it turning into blood. Even with these wonders at his disposal, Moses continues to come up with reasons why he is not the man for the job. In Exodus 4:10-12, Moses is telling the Lord that he is slow of speech or that he has a speech impediment. I can only imagine that this would have been a source of great shame and embarrassment for Moses growing up, and it is the exact weakness that the Lord wanted to show Himself strong in.

    How powerful would it have been for the pharaoh who grew up watching Moses struggle to speak, now sees him standing in the courtroom of Egypt speaking clearly and with authority? Y'shua even offers to speak for him in verse 12, "Now go! **I AM** (Anokhi)! I will be with your mouth and I will teach you what you will say." Y'shua wanted Moses to be one of His wonders! However, Moses was still unable to receive the blessing that God had for him, and instead begged that the Lord would send Aaron to be his speaker. Moses traded God's voice for Aaron's! When is the last time that the Lord has called you to do something that had the potential to expose your greatest weakness? Our first response is often the thought that the Lord is trying to humiliate us, or whatever other lie the enemy may attack you with. In 2 Corinthians 12:9, Paul writes "And He spoke to me, 'My grace is sufficient for you, for My power is made complete in weakness.' Therefore I shall gladly boast more in my weakness, so that the power of the Messiah would take possession with me." Y'shua wanted to show His complete power in Moses' weakness by speaking through him. There is a reason why the Lord wants to use your weaknesses, sometimes even more so than you strengths. It is because He wants you to be one of His wonders; by doing so, not only will you declare who Christ is, but you will realize that, in Christ, you have no weaknesses! You only have areas in your life where He is glorified, and other areas in your life where Christ is glorified even more.

Glory in hardship

The time has finally come: the bride that has been held captive for over four hundred years will see her groom in all of His Glory. There is not a romantic action thriller on the big screen or in novel form that can compare to this. The Lord has been eagerly waiting for this time when he could show Himself mighty; and He is sending a man who stutters and his brother who has served false gods for most of his life to proclaim His love to His people. However, in Exodus 4:21 we see what appears to be the Lord working against what He called Moses to do. The passage reads "And the Lord said to Moses, 'When you return to Egypt, see that you do before Pharaoh all those miracles and wonders which I have put in your hand; but I will make him stubborn and harden his heart, so that he will let the people go." On the surface, this does not make any sense. Why would God tell Moses to stand against Pharaoh with the miracles He has given him, and then turn around and harden Pharaoh's heart? The reason is that the Lord's goal was not Pharaoh's heart, but the hearts of the Israelites. If Moses would have asked Pharaoh to let the children of Israel go and make sacrifices to the Lord in the wilderness; and Pharaoh agreed without any resistance, the Israelites would have left and come right back. This may seem like a stretch; however, the children of Israel have seen the Egyptians prospering under their gods and they (Israel) may have very well forgotten the faithfulness of their God.

    The Lord was giving Himself the opportunity to prove His love to His people through hardship. In the story of Lazarus in John 11, Mary (who anointed Y'shua with perfume and wiped His feet) sent for Y'shua saying that her brother was sick and needed Him. In verse 4 we read, "When Y'shua received the message, He said, 'This sickness is not to end in death; but [on the contrary] it is to honor God and to promote His Glory, that the Son of God may be glorified through (by) it." Just as we would question how the Lord would be glorified through the hardening of Pharaoh's heart; I am sure the same question went through Mary's mind with the death of Lazarus. Especially after what we read in verse 6, "Therefore [even] when He heard that Lazarus was sick, He still stayed two days longer in the same place where He was."

    This decision pretty much sealed Lazarus' fate, just as the hardening of Pharaoh's heart would almost certainly do the same for Israel. However, Joe Amaral in his book "*Understanding Jesus*" gives us an amazing insight into the Hebrew culture that shows what Y'shua was really up to. During the time of Christ, there was a belief that once a person died, their soul hovered over the body for three days. When the third day had past, resurrection was impossible because the soul had gone to its final and permanent resting place. It was also the belief during that time that only the Messiah could raise someone after three days. So Y'shua didn't stay two extra days because He was indifferent to Lazarus' condition; rather, He was allowing a hardship to set the stage for His glory, so the people could see Him for who He really was. If He had simply healed Lazarus before he died, this would not have declared who Christ was since healing was not uncommon during this time. It is the exact same desire that the Lord had for Israel: for there to be the opportunity for His children to see with their own eyes the greatness of their

God. I never thought of my hardships as opportunities for God to show me who He really is. In my flesh, I just assumed that the Lord was angry with me or that I was being punished for some sin. But what if we truly believed that the Lord has intended good no matter what weapon the enemy brings against us? And that the hardship could be setting the stage for not only our healing or deliverance, but so we may know Him in a way we have never seen before. Jeremiah 29:11 says "For I know the thoughts and plans that I have for you, said the Lord, thoughts and plans for welfare and peace and not for evil, to give you hope in your final outcome." Some translations say "to prosper you and not to harm you;" but when we go through hardships, it can easily begin to feel like harm. Merriam-Webster.com defines harm as "physical or mental damage or injury: something that causes someone or something to be hurt, broken, made less valuable or successful." Therefore, harm, by definition, is done with the sole intent of causing injury or decreasing value and nothing else, and the Lord is telling us that this is not His heart. His "hurt" brings growth, brokenness which causes healing, and drives us to seek Him more earnestly. A great example of this is the difference between a knife in the hand of a murderer, and a knife in the hand of a surgeon. One desires to cause pain and to ruin lives, but the other has to cause harm as well. However, the surgeon causes harm to bring healing and to get to what is killing you. The scars left by an attacker can cause very painful memories, but the scars left by a surgeon bring the comfort that what was wrong has finally been made right.

The enemy knows this to be true, and it is why he starts trying to get us to blame God when trials and tribulations come. If he can get us to forget just how much we are adored by God, then it will be very easy for us to believe that the Lord does not have our best interest in mind. Moses and Aaron would soon see this first hand in the hearts of the Israelites. When Moses and Aaron tell Pharaoh to let the children of Israel go, Pharaoh becomes enraged and forces the children of Israel to make bricks without straw. But the Lord reminds Moses that he would delivers Israel with all of His wonders, and that all of Egypt would know that He is the One true living God.

Yehovah the Redeemer

If the promise of deliverance and a tremendous show of power wasn't enough, the Lord takes it a step further and shows a side of Himself that even Moses' forefathers had not seen before. In Exodus 6:2-3 we read, "And God said to Moses, I am the Lord. And I appeared to Abraham, to Isaac, and to Jacob by My name El Shaddia (God Almighty), But I was not known to them by My name Lord [Yehovah-the redemptive name of God] (One New Man Bible, explanation of Lord from the Amplified Bible)." Abraham, Isaac, and Jacob saw the faithfulness of God in

His ability to keep them and His promises to them, but it is Moses that gets to see the Lord in the way that we ourselves know Him. However, before the Lord can save a nation, He must first destroy their gods. As I said before, Israel has spent generations waiting for God to move and the Lord needed to reestablish who He was in their hearts. The first Egyptian god that the Lord set His sights on was "Hapi," god of the Nile. In Exodus 7:20-21 we read, "Moses and Aaron did as the Lord commanded; Aaron lifted up the rod and smote the waters in the river in the sight of Pharaoh and his servants; and all the waters in the river were turned to blood. And the fish in the river died; and the river became foul smelling, and the Egyptians could not drink its water, and there was blood throughout all the land of Egypt." Everything the Lord does have a specific purpose and nothing done is wasted. For the first time, a vital source of life and water for Egypt was devastated and "Hapi" was silent. Even the Egyptian god "Ra" (God of the Sun) was not immune to the Lord's power. For three days it was as dark as night and no matter how hard the Egyptian priests prayed and worshiped, Ra's silence spoke volumes. I can't imagine the joy and hope this must have brought to the Jewish people.

    After centuries of holding on to glimmers of hope, their God was flexing His power for all to see. In all of my favorite movies, the hero/heroine spends most of the time enduring ridicule, failure, doubt, and hardship. Then, the moment he/she has been waiting for comes, and the hero/heroine breaks through with incredible strength, courage, and skill to do the impossible. Suddenly, all who doubt or were cautiously optimistic finds themselves breathless and inspired to greatness themselves.

I have often wondered why Pharaoh even allowed Moses to come to him so freely. During that time, Pharaoh had to power to kill whomever he wished without any reason at all and Moses would have known that. If you go back a few verses to Exodus 7:1-2, we see some very interesting wording that once again shows God's heart: "And the Lord said to Moses, 'See I have made you a **god** to Pharaoh, and Aaron your brother will be your prophet. You will speak all that I command you and Aaron your brother will speak to Pharaoh, so he will send the children of Israel out of his land." On the surface, this scripture seems to contradict the Word that there are no other gods besides the God of Abraham, Isaac, and Jacob.

I liked the way that William Moford described this passage of scripture when he said, "The word here is *elohim*, not referring to the Elohim, but still plural! It is the God in Moses that makes Pharaoh respect Moses. God will never abandon of forsake anyone, but those whose hearts are tuned to Him operate in His perfect will with boldness and confidence." This task would have been impossible for Moses to accomplish on his own, and the anger of Pharaoh would have more than likely gotten Moses an Aaron killed. Also during that time, the Pharaoh was seen as god incarnate who was to be feared and worshiped. So if Moses had favor with Pharaoh the way that he did, that means that the presence of God was so heavy on Moses that Pharaoh looked upon him as an equal...a man with "God-like authority." This is the closeness that the Lord wants to have in our lives, that we would walk with such power and authority to do what He has called us to do that we appear "Christ-like."

Though this time must have brought great excitement to the Jewish people, I can also see how the sheer power of His might could be a fearful thing as well. Especially when the Egyptian people began dying and crying out from their afflictions. Even then, the Lord brings His people comfort in the form of a Psalm. In Psalms 91:1, 3, and 7 we read, "He who dwells in the secret place of the Most High will abide under the shadow of the Almighty...3) Surely He will deliver you from the snare of the fowler and from the destructive pestilence...7) A thousand may fall at your side and ten thousand at your right hand, but it will not come near you." There have been so many times in my life when I have gone through physical, spiritual, or emotional hardship and I have cried out to the Lord for deliverance. Time and again in His mercy, He would give me a Word that would not stop the circumstances, but rather it would change my perspective of the situation and my ability to endure it. When I would begin to fear my situation or doubt His faithfulness, I found that Y'shua had not changed, only my perception of Him had changed. When Israel sat and watched the wrath of God being poured out on Egypt, I imagine that they too became fearful that they would have to endure the same hardship.

God had not changed, only their perception of Him had changed as they saw a new side to His love and character.

    Despite the Lord's incredible show of strength and superiority, Pharaoh's heart remained hardened and would not let the children of Israel go. So the Lord would soon unleash the final plague in the form of killing all of the first-born of Egypt, starting with Pharaoh's son. However, before this was done the Lord commanded Moses to kill a lamb, dipped hyssop in its blood, and strike it on the lintel (top) and the two side posts on the door of his house. He also commanded Moses to tell the children of Israel to do the same (Exodus 12:21-28). The question I have is, out of all of the plagues that fell upon Egypt, why do the children of Israel need to protect themselves from this one? Couldn't the Lord simply withhold His hand from them as He did with the other 9 plagues? What's even more interesting about this commandment is in verse 24 we read, "And you will observe this thing for an ordinance for you and your sons forever." Needless to say, this commandment is slightly important to the Lord, so there must be more to it than simply placing lamb's blood on a door. Joe Amaral noted that by placing the blood on the door post in this manner is to write a "letter of Blood," the children of Israel were writing the 8th letter of the Hebrew alphabet which is "chet." "Chet" means "life!"

    What a beautiful picture the Lord is painting here, that where life is, death cannot enter. When Christ was crucified, He bled from His hands and His crown of thorns, which fits this word picture being painted in the Passover commandment. If that weren't enough, in John 10:9, Y'shua declares "I AM the Door: if someone would enter through Me he will be saved and he will enter and he will go out and he will find the pasture." Halleluiah! Not only was the Lord making a way of escape for Israel from this final plague (and I believe giving them their first test in trusting Him), but He was again setting the stage for His son so future generations would have a point of reference when Christ died as to what He was really doing.

    Just as the Lord did with Abraham and Sarah, the bride was freed from captivity and the spoils of her captor went with her. The Bible says that the children of Israel left with the wealth of Egypt and that Moses was very great in the land. (Exodus 11:2-3) So far, the children of Israel have seen the Lord as El Shaddia (God Almighty) and Yaweh (God our Deliverer), but now they will be forced to trust in His provision and His leadership. As many of us who have been there before know, there is a certain kind of love, trust, and intimacy with the Lord that can only be found in the wilderness.

Chapter 5

Trust Me

Ask any self-professing Christian if they trust God, and a majority of them will give you the knee jerk (and many times preprogrammed) response of an enthusiastic "Yes!" Yet, of the potentially 9 out of 10 who say "yes" without hesitation, there is that one percent that will honestly tell you that they don't as much as they should. Positive confessions and confessions of faith are a wonderful thing, but so is being real with yourself and with the Lord. I remember my mother telling me one time when I was younger, "James, you need to check your heart and find out the difference between what you know and what you believe." Our heads can hold a tremendous amount of Biblical knowledge, but if that is where it stops, then we are simply well-educated unbelievers. Such were the hearts of the nations that the Lord was trying to win and create into His people Israel. I say "nations" because Israel was not the only nationality that left Egypt on the day of deliverance. The children of Israel had married with other nations in Egypt that were in slavery as well, which we see in Exodus 12:38, "And a mixed multitude also went up with them, and flocks and herds, very many cattle." So the Lord had to contest with those who knew Him while they were amongst those who did not. Knowing this, the

Lord took the children of Israel by way of the Reed Sea instead of going through the land of the Philistines.

Even though the children of Israel came out of Egypt armed, the Lord was concerned that war would change their hearts and cause them to return to Egypt (Exodus 13:17). So instead of the Lord throwing them head long into overwhelming circumstances, He considered their hearts and decided to use this opportunity to demonstrate His love once again. As the children of Israel travelled, Exodus 13:21 says "And the Lord went before them by day in a pillar of cloud to lead them the way, and by night in a pillar of fire, to give them light, to go by day and night." If you remember we read that when Solomon dedicated the temple on the eighth and greatest day of the feast; and later on in the Gospels, John records that on the eighth and greatest day of the feast Christ declared that He was the light of the world. By doing this, Christ was declaring that he was the light that filled the temple in the form of a thick cloud! So it is not too far of a stretch to assume that the pillar of cloud by day and the pillar of fire by night was Christ leading His people, just like a Good Shepherd leading His flock to green pastures. What a beautiful picture! This wasn't just millions of people wandering aimlessly into the Egyptian wilderness, but the fold of God being guided every step of the way.

In Exodus 14:1, we see the Lord tell Moses to speak to the children of Israel and tell them to "turn" and camp near Pi Hakhirot. By doing this, the Lord is telling Israel to go back towards the Egyptian army that they will soon find is pursuing them. Just as the Lord told Jacob to go back and face Esau, this decision must have seemed more like suicide. However, even though it seems like the Lord was using live bait to draw Egypt in, I believe that He wanted His children to have a front row seat to His faithfulness. The Lord could have destroyed the Egyptian army before they even left their gate, but He didn't. He could have caused them to be lost in the wilderness or conceal Israel's tracks, but He instead chose to allow Egypt to come barreling down on them with all of their military might. More food for thought: how did Pharaoh know that the Israelites didn't pass through Philistine territory, but rather they went the way of the Reed Sea? Could it be that the Lord (who the Bible says in Exodus 14:17 "...strengthen the hearts of the Egyptians") led Pharaoh to where the children of Israel were camped? So why would the Lord cause this to happen? The answer is contained later on in this same passage of scripture which reads, "...and they will follow them and I shall get honor for Myself from Pharaoh, and from his whole army, his chariots, and his horseman." Pharaoh just knew that he had Israel right where he wanted them, and that they had either returned to Egypt or he would run them down like grass. Little did he know, he and his men were pawns in the Lord's plan to show Israel that they could trust Him, and that nothing was impossible for their God.

As the Egyptians drew closer, the children of Israel (like so many of us do) began cursing their freedom and began longing for the bondage they once screamed for deliverance from. I love this display of God's heart. He could have easily grown indignant towards Israel after all He did to bring them to this point; instead, He chooses to defend them despite their lack of faith. I can think of many times in my life where the Lord has called me to a place that I just knew was meant for my harm. "Lord, this couldn't possibly be your plan," I would say. "If I do this, I risk losing things that I love. I risk embarrassment, shame, ridicule, and I don't even see how I get any glory out of it!" In spite of my kicking and screaming, I would do what the Lord asked me to do and opposition would quickly come. When I moved away from South Carolina where my parents were to live near my soon to be wife, my family was convinced that this was not what God would have for me.

My beautiful Alicia at the time was a recently divorced single mother of three, who had survived a very physically and verbally abusive marriage. On top of that, in order to be with her, I had to sell my truck, drop out of the University of South Carolina, and break the lease on my apartment. Does any of this sound like a good idea so far? Now keep in mind, Alicia and I were friends from when I used to live in California; we met in church, and I was the first person to sign her guest list at her engagement party to her first husband (gotta love God's sense of humor). So here I was in California with only the clothes on my back and I had to live with my soon to be in-laws. How's that for a crash course in getting to know family?

Yet, despite all of the fear, uncertainty, the doubt, and the many hardships that came shortly afterwards, the Lord defended me and guided me every step of the way. Alicia and I have now been married for 7 years, we have 6 children, and I cannot imagine my life any other way. When we are obedient to the Lord's calling and direction, He will deliver and defend us with the same passion and intensity as He did Israel. Exodus 14:19 says that "And the angle of God (Christ), who went before the camp of Israel, removed and went behind them, and the pillar of the cloud went from before their face and stood behind them." (Christ added) Just to reiterate what I said earlier in reference to the belief that "angel of God" or "The angel of the Lord" being Christ. It is believed, which I believe also, that when the writers of the Old Testament saw Christ appear to them, they did not know who He was or what to call him.

This makes sense because Isaiah at this point had not yet written his prophecy that Christ would be called Wonderful, Counselor, Emanuel, Prince of Peace, Mighty God. (Isaiah 9:5) However, they were able to make the observation that He was higher in authority than all of the angels, and He was not named in scripture such as the angel Michael or Gabriel. This belief in no way suggests that Y'shua is an angel, for we know that, threw Him, all things were created and without Him nothing was created.

This belief simply reaffirms the fact that Y'shua has been an intricate part of God's plan from the beginning, and He has played a very active role the whole time.

You'll notice in this passage that the Good Shepherd that was once leading His sheep is now defending them against harm. What a beautiful picture of how our God leads us today; He is declaring that He will never take us to a place that He Himself is not able and willing to defend. If you are familiar with this historical account, you know that Moses prayed all night and that the sea parted in front of Israel. Even the water that was in the sea bed parted so they could walk on dry land! The Egyptian army pursued after them and the Bible says that, as they did, "...the Lord looked at the army of the Egyptians through the pillar of fire and of cloud, and caused confusion with the army of the Egyptians, and took off their chariot wheels, so they drove them heavily so that the Egyptians said, 'Let us flee from the face of the Israel, for the Lord is fighting for them against the Egyptians." (Exodus 14:24-25) The Lord took off their chariot wheels?! Not only did the Lord bring the enemy of Israel into a trap, He then made it so that there was no escape for them. There should be an overwhelming sense of joy that comes upon us when we realize that not only will the Lord take out any enemy that comes against us, but He will also make it so that this enemy has no possible chance of escape! William Mofford summed it up best when he said, "Commentary says that Moses called to

Pharaoh on the western side of the sea. 'You asked Who the Lord was. Now you know. (ONMB p. 108)"

Be near oh God:

Once Israel left Egypt, they camped in the wilderness near Mount Sinai, and this is where the Lord would truly introduce Himself to His people. Up until this point, the Lord has spoken exclusively with Moses and then Moses would in turn tell the people what God has commanded. If the fact that He wanted to now speak to His people wasn't incredible enough, the way He chose to do it was even more amazing. In the video documentary "Know Your Enemy" by The Fuel Project which I have referred to earlier, there is a direct link between mountains and God. For 430 years, the Pyramids were the mountains that the children of Israel saw and Pharaoh was the "god" that sat on top of them. This visual example was to declare to the people that he had dominion and absolute rule over what he created. Seeing how Israel was in Egypt for so many years, this would have been a concept they were very familiar with.

The tower of Babel and later on Zeus and Mount Olympus were all based off of these "Mysteries" (which became known as the Babylonian Mysteries) belief system as well. Knowing this, it should be no surprise where the

Lord took the children of Israel so that He could properly introduce Himself…..a mountain. Exodus 19:16-20 reads, "And it was on the third day in the morning that there were thunders and lightning and a thick cloud upon the mountain, and the sound of the shofar was exceedingly loud, so that all the people in the camp trembled. And Moses brought the people out of the camp to meet with God and they stood at the base of the mountain. And Mount Sinai was altogether in smoke, because the Lord descended upon it in fire and its smoke ascended like the smoke of a furnace, and the whole mountain quaked greatly. And when the sound of the shofar sounded long and grew louder and louder, Moses spoke and God answered him audibly. And the Lord came down upon Mount Sinai, on the top of the mountain and the Lord called Moses up to the top of the mountain, and Moses went up." I am willing to bet that the children of Israel never saw Pharaoh do this to the pyramids.

What an introduction! The Lord wanted Israel to have no doubt in their minds as to Who they were following and the power of His hand. This also takes all of the steam out of the beliefs that God only speaks to one person, and then it is up to that one person to tell His people what He thinks of them. Granted, the people were only allowed to come to the base of the mountain while Moses went up to speak with God; but God could not simply bring the people of Israel into the same level of relationship as He had with Moses. Just like with the burning bush, the Lord had to first demonstrate His power to Moses, and Who He was before He could begin the process of establishing a relationship with him.

      Having given Moses the Ten Statements (it is believed that the Lord wrote the entire Torah on the tablets), the Lord then gives Moses instructions on how to build a location where He can meet with His people...the Tabernacle. Again, we see the Lord wanting to move past simply meeting with Moses alone, to having a place where the Lord could be tangibly near those He loved so much. If you really stop and think about what the Lord is doing here, it should absolutely blow your mind! The Lord of Heaven and Earth is more content with being in a small structure built by His children, than to reign from on high in the beauty and perfection of Heaven. He then <u>asked</u>, not commanded, but asked that the children of Israel to provide the materials for His dwelling place. Exodus 25:2 says, "Speak to the children of Israel, that they will bring Me an offering: you will take My offering from every man who gives it <u>willingly</u> with his heart. (Emphasis added)" Up to this point, the Lord has been showing His children His might, His power, and His protection; but now the Lord has taken the position of wanting to receive love. It is as if the Lord wants to see what affect His actions have had on His people, and if they want Him near. What an incredible thought that God not only IS love, but He longs for our love as well! For those of you who struggle with not feeling worthy to even come near to Him as I do some times, this truth should liberate us from that lie of the enemy. You are adored by Majesty, and our jealous God has gone above and beyond so that we might be able to draw near to Him. The Lord could have easily created His own dwelling place, and it could have been more breathtaking than anything we have ever seen. Masterpieces can be awe inspiring and the skill of the artists seem almost super human, receiving one would be no less breath taking. Yet in all honesty, can it really compare to your young child handing you a piece of paper, with two stick figures scribbled on it, and written on the top of the page is "you and me, I love you." You know that there are much better artists out there, but this was created as an act of love by someone that you adore. It is the willing act of love that makes the drawing priceless. I believe the Lord had the same concept in mind when He asked the children of Israel to create a place for Him with a willing heart.

    Next the Lord told Moses to craft The Ark made of acacia wood overlaid with gold. The Bible goes into elaborate detail as to how it would be crafted, including the figures of the Cherubim angels and the length of the acacia poles that would carry it. It is estimated that the Ark of the Covenant weighed anywhere from 1500-2000lbs, which would have been far more weight than the rods or the four priests could bear. Inside the Ark was Aaron's rod that bloomed, the ashes of a red heifer, a bowl of mana, and the Ten Statements (or Torah). All of these were reminders of God's faithfulness to Israel, and all who saw the priest carrying the Ark knew the Lord Himself was bearing the load. Even in the wilderness, Y'shua was providing us a visual example of His words in Matthew

11:28-30 "Come to Me all those who work and are burdened, and I shall give you rest. You must immediately take My yoke upon you and you must now learn from Me, because I am gentle and humble in My heart, and you will find rest for your lives: for my yoke is pleasant (or light) and My burden is insignificant." The word "insignificant" here suggests that His burden is so light, you won't even realize that you are carrying it. How amazing it must have been to be one of the priests that picked up the Ark for the first time. I imagine they must have almost thrown it through the top of the tent anticipating its weight to be unbearable. However, it is the combination of both the Tabernacle and the Ark of the Covenant that created an entirely new concept for Moses and the children of Israel: the ability to abide in His presence.

    I heard a study by Pastor Mark Biltz on the Haftarah "Terumah" (meaning something set apart for a free-will gift), in which he describes the Hebrew word "Yod" (or power of God) and how the symbol of the Yod looks like a hook. Pastor Biltz said that the Yods were placed in the Torah to give the appearance as if they are linking the scriptures together, and they were displaying God's word like the curtains of the Tabernacle. Knowing that the Word of God is Christ, the Lord was giving Moses specific instructions on how to craft yet another visible representation of His Son. From Exodus 25-40, the Lord describes not only how the Tabernacle is to be made, but how the priests would have to prepare before they could enter in. After you read these fifteen lengthy and detail-oriented chapters, I want you to picture this: everything you just read is now inside you! When you receive Y'shua as your Savior, His Spirit lives with your heart, making it the Holy of Holies. All your wounds, the filth, and shame of your sins are replaced with gold, silver, bronze, blue, purple, scarlet, and fine linen. The Lord takes what is broken and turns it into something Holy for Him to dwell in. Y'shua reinforces this in John 15:4, "Dwell in Me, and I will dwell in you. [Live in me, and I will live in you.] Just as no branch can bear fruit of itself without abiding in (being vitally united to) the vine, neither can you bear fruit unless you abide in Me." (Amplified Bible) This whole concept and understanding of abiding in Him and He in us stems from the Tabernacle. What an amazing thought that He had His children create a place for Him so He could be close, and so later on we could understand what it means to live in Him.

On a side note: the word "Holy" does not mean "perfect" and the opposite of Holy does not mean sin. The word Holy means something that it set apart, so if something is "unholy," then it is common. If you had fine China plates that were worth thousands of dollar, would you place a cheeseburger or cereal in it? Of course not! The reason why this strikes us as a silly question is because we realize that the China is "special;" or in Biblical terms, "Holy" and these items are considered common. The Lord could not have had this deep of a relationship with Israel in Egypt, where "common gods" and common things were worshiped. He wanted them to be "Holy" or set apart from

Egypt and all other nations. He made a covenant with them and gave them His Words which no one else had. When the Lord calls us to be Holy, He is not calling us into a life of perfection or robotic obedience. He is calling us to be set apart; He is calling us to a place where He can dwell with us and us with Him. With this understanding of Holiness, walking in the calling of God in Romans 12:1-2 seems to have a greater meaning than simply "not sinning." "Therefor I urge you, brothers, through the compassion of God, to present your bodies as <u>holy</u>, living offerings, pleasing to God, your spiritual service: and stop being conformed to this age, but you must from the inside continually be changed into another form, by the renovation of your mind, to prove what is good and pleasing and perfect will of God for you." Notice that the Lord didn't say that you were to be perfect; He said that His will for you is perfect. The ways of this world are common and the Lord is calling us to a life that is uncommon:"holy." Y'shua knows the beauty that He has already created in you, so do not settle for ordinary when He has called you to be extraordinary. The Holy of Holies dwells within you!

<u>Washing away the past:</u>

After spending four hundred and thirty years under pagan rule, I can only imagine the spiritual baggage the children of Israel must have been carrying. Night and day they would have heard the prayers, the worship, and seen the offering made to idols and felt the demonic oppression that came with it. In order for the Lord to have a people set apart for Himself both physically and spiritually, He had to cleanse them and teach them the steps to purify themselves. This process is well-known as "Sanctification;" and for most of us, it can seem like a bunch of rules to follow or mindless traditions. However, I love how Merriam-Webster.com defines the word "Sanctify," and I believe it brings clarity as to why this process was so important to the Lord. It says, "To set apart to a sacred purpose, to free from sin, to impart or impute sacredness inviolability, or respect." This was what the Lord wanted for His people; to be sacred, to be free from sin, and to be respected because of the relationship they had with the Living God.

You see this process being described in Exodus 29 with the sanctifying of Aaron and his sons. Yet, the part that strikes me the most in this chapter is where the Lord commands Aaron and his sons to place their hands on the heads of bulls and rams while they are being sacrificed. There was a belief during this time that when a person brought a sin offering to the preist, they would place their hands on the head of the sacrifice, while it was being killed, and their sin would be passed on to the animal. As we have seen so many times before, the Lord was giving His children a process that would later declare Y'shua and give greater revelation into Who He was.

Fast-forward to the crucifixion of Christ and we see this very same act played out. In Luke 22:63-65 we read, "And the men holding Him were mocking and beating Him, then after they blindfolded Him they were asking Him saying, 'You must prophesy now, who is the one who hit you?' And they were saying many other blasphemous things to Him." What an incredible thought that every time they struck Christ, He was taking their sin upon Himself as a sin offering!

<u>Faithful when we fall:</u>

I have heard people argue that if the same God of love that we know in the New Testament existed in the Old, then why did he kill/punish so many of His own? What about the plagues and the wondering forty years in the wilderness? Though these are very valid questions, there are two questions I would ask in return to help put the Lord's actions into a better perspective. First, what was the Lord looking to accomplish through His actions? And secondly, how much of the Lord's wrath was NOT unleashed upon His people? God's heart becomes pretty clear when you consider His incredible level of restraint. Take the golden calf for example in Exodus 31-32. Moses ascends Mount Sinai once again to speak to the Lord face-to-face and to receive His Torah. Moses is delayed on the mountain for forty days and the people began to grow impatient. So they approach Aaron and ask him to make them false gods since they do not know if Moses is still alive. In Exodus 32:2-4 we read, "And Aaron said to them, 'Take off the golden earrings, which are in the ears of your wives, of your sons, and of your daughters and bring them to me.' And all the people took off the golden earrings, which were in their ears and brought them to Aaron. And he took them from their hand and fashioned it in a mold, and he made a molten calf and they said, 'This is your God, O Israel, that brought you up out of the land of Egypt." The sin of Israel and Aaron in this single act must have wounded the Lord's heart on so many levels.

    First, where did Israel get the gold earrings to give to Aaron? They used the gold that the Lord caused Egypt to give to them as a blessing when they were freed from their bondage. Secondly, what was the animal that Aaron chose to make an idol out of? The image of the calf (or bull) was used by the Mysteries belief system to represent Nimrod. Nimrod was one of the founders of this pagan belief system which was prevalent in Egypt while Israel was there. Finally, Israel then dared to sing praises to the calf (Nimrod) and say that IT was the one who brought them out of the land of Egypt! After all the plagues they saw with their own eyes, the wealth that was given to them, walking across an ocean on dry land, and their enemy being consumed by that same ocean. Then being provided for while in the wilderness, and being given the blueprints on how to build a structure so they might draw near to the God who loved them so much; they still chose another over Him. With this understanding of the level of blasphemy that Israel willingly participated in, it is easy to see why the Lord's wrath was kindled so greatly against His people. In Exodus 32:8 we read, " They have turned aside quickly out of the Way which I commanded them: they have made themselves a molten calf and have worshiped it and sacrificed to it and said, 'This is your God, O Israel, that has brought you out of the land of Egypt." The fact that the Lord quotes what Israel was saying while they worshiped the calf, tells me that He was in their midst while they were doing it.

So it wasn't just that the Lord learned about what Israel was doing; He saw with His own eyes and heard it with His own ears. To summarize God's plan later on in this chapter, He tells Moses to leave Him alone so He can wipe out Israel and then make a mighty nation out of Moses. The Lord was ready to kill millions of people and start anew with Moses one generation at a time as He did with Abraham! Amazingly enough, the Lord allows Moses to reason with Him just like He let Abraham when He was planning to destroy Sodom and Gomorra.

The conversation that Moses has in response to the Lord's anger shows just how deep their relationship went. In Exodus 32:11-14 we read, "And Moses sought the Lord his God and said, 'Lord, why does Your wrath wax hot against Your people, whom you have brought out of the land of Egypt with great power and with a mighty hand? Why should the Egyptians speak and say, He brought them out for evil, to slay them in the mountains and to consume them from the face of the earth? Turn from Your fierce wrath and be sorry of this evil against Your people. Remember Abraham, Isaac, and Israel, Your servants, to whom you did swear by Your own self and said to them, I shall multiply your seed as the stars of Heaven, and all this land that I have spoken of will I give to your seed, and they will inherit it forever.' And the Lord was sorry for the evil which He thought to do to His people." Look at the level of boldness that the Lord allows Moses to speak to Him with, and keep in mind that this conversation was taking place face-to-face with creator of the known Universe! First off, Moses asked the Lord why He was so angry with Israel. After describing earlier the multiple levels of blasphemy that Israel had committed in this single act, how on earth can Moses ask God "why does Your wrath wax hot against Your people?" It is almost as if Moses is reminding the Lord that the children of Israel are merely babes in Him, and they do not know what they are doing. We see this child-like behavior in the way that Israel proclaimed that the calf had delivered them out of Egypt, when we know full well that it was God alone who saved them.

    I see this same kind of behavior in my five-year-old daughter Eliana. Like when it was her birthday and she told her younger sister Shoshanah, "Daddy said that the birthday cake is mine and no one else can have any!" Needless to say, her statement was far from accurate and there is no way I would say such a thing. So Moses is asking the Lord to write off the horrible claim that the calf delivered Israel, as being no more than the senseless comments of children. Moses then asked the Lord to consider His actions for His namesake. This is so powerful in that Moses is asking the Lord how Egypt (and the world for that matter) will know of His faithfulness and provision for His people if He kills them all. Finally, Moses reminds the Lord of the covenant that He made with Abraham, Isaac, and Israel. Notice that Moses didn't call the man Israel by his name of Jacob, he wanted to remind the Lord of when He wrestled and changed Jacob's name to Israel. I believe that Moses wanted the Lord not to see Israel as a stiff neck people, but as His servant Jacob whom He blessed. Yet, the most jaw dropping part of this whole conversation is the Lord's response to it. The Lord willingly concedes to Moses' plea, He extends His limitless mercy towards Israel, and the Word even goes so far as to say that He was sorry for the evil that He thought towards His people. The mercy of our God is without end!

    Once again, we see the Lord allowing Himself to be reasoned with the same way He did with Abraham. I believe the Lord wanted to show Moses the level of relationship that he could have with Him, and to test the leadership qualities in his heart towards Israel. Would Moses be in agreement with the Lord's plan, or would he intercede on their behalf? Sound familiar? In Romans 8:33-34, we read, "Who will accuse against the chosen people of God? God is the righteous One: who is the one who condemns? Certainly not Messiah Y'shua the One who died, but rather, has risen, and Who is on the right hand of

God, and Who is interceding on our behalf." Even while they are in blatant sin, the Lord's heart is moved by the cries of one man. When I read this portion of scripture, I can see Moses' actions being a foreshadowing of Christ. To take this picture of Christ even further, we see the Word in the form of the Commandments coming down from the mountain of God to a people in sin, and the righteous being separated from the unjust. This entire scripture plays out the same way that the Word describes Christ's return for His church! If this wasn't enough, Exodus 32:21, Moses returns to the camp, speaks on the Lord's behalf, and says "And Moses said to Aaron, 'What did this people do to you that you have brought so great a sin upon them?" The word "sin" used here means an act done against God **by accident**! For us, we would consider this a "transgression" which is sin done with the intention of angering God. Yet, as He did on the cross, the Lord forgives them for they know not what they do.

God's plan revealed:

In the next chapter, we will be moving onto the book of Numbers where we see yet a new dynamic of God's heart come to light. Before we do, I wanted to touch on something incredible in Leviticus that I myself nearly missed. There are a tremendous amount of commandments on how to handle nearly every aspect of daily life for the children of Israel. From offerings, oaths, and touching unclean things, to circumcisions and purification, this book can seem rather tedious to read (especially if you do not have a strong background in the Hebrew language and the symbolism of what was being done, which I will freely admit that I do not). However, Leviticus chapter 23 has been referred to as "God's calendar of redeeming grace" or "the calendar of divine redemption." This may seem a little confusing when you first open to this chapter in your Bible and find that it is all about the Lord's feasts. I am willing to go out on a limb and say that the feasts are the greatest proclamation of who Christ is in the entire Bible. A very strong statement, I know; if it is true (which I hope to demonstrate), wouldn't it make sense why the enemy would attack this section of the Bible (Torah) and try to convenience the church that its contents have been "done away with?"

    If you are a believer in Christ, you know from both study and personal experience that Y'shua is the Son of God. We know that He is the Messiah that the world has been waiting for and that salvation is solely found in Him. But even then, I have had people of other faiths try to sway me to their belief by either writing off my experiences with God, or by trying to persuade me through their own "version" of the Bible. This has brought about confusion and frustration in the past, especially when it comes to differences in denominations. At the end of the day, I am left asking myself the question "who has it right?" Is it the Baptist, the Pentecostals, the Evangelicals, the Methodist, the Lutherans? And the list goes on and on until you are left wondering if it is at all possible for anyone to have an accurate approach to the Word of God. As I have mentioned earlier in this book, I believe that the confusion has come from the church discarding the foundation of the Word, and we are left "stabbing in the dark" for truth. I know the Lord saw this coming, and that is why He laid out His plan for what He was going to do right from the beginning. It was just cleverly hidden in the feasts all this time; there are Orthodox Jews all over the world celebrating their Savior every year and they don't even realize it.

In the first chapter of this book, I mentioned the Hebrew word for "feast" was Mo'ed and that it meant "divine appointment." Amazingly enough, the Bible said that these feasts are to be a "Holy Convocation" meaning a large gathering of people in a public place or "dress rehearsal." When I first heard that the Feasts were dress rehearsals, the question that came to my mind was "what were they rehearsing for?" Then through personal study and from some of the great works I reference to Mark Biltz and Joe Amaral, the revelation hit me square in the heart. They were practicing Christ's coming! The first Feast given was the Feast of Pesach or Passover which we briefly discussed in Exodus. The children were to take a spotless lamb, and slay it in public; they were not to break a single bone, and their salvation from the angel of death would be found in the blood. As you can see already, this first feast describes in profound detail the price that Christ was going to pay. But, for the sake of argument, lets dive into this even further. Fast forwarding to the time of Christ, only a High Priest of Israel was allowed to select the spotless lamb for the Passover sacrifice. So if Y'shua was the sacrificial lamb as Paul describes Him in 1 Corinthians 5:7, then what high priest selected Christ to be the sacrifice? What is the answer? John the Baptist. If you remember from the first chapter of Luke, John's father Zachariah was a priest and of the division of Abijah. Zachariah's wife (Elizabeth) was a Levite and was named after Aaron's wife, and you can't be more in the lineage of Aaron than these two. So John was a high priest of Israel by birth and carried that authority. We find this declaration in John 1:29, "The next day he (John the Baptist) saw Y'shua coming toward him and said, 'Behold, the Lamb of God, the One Who takes away the sin of the world."

The next is the feast of Unleavened Bread, which is where the Lord commands Israel to eat bread without leaven for seven days. The leaven is a representation of sin, so Matzah bread is commonly eaten during this time. If you have seen a piece of Matzah bread before, it is flat with brown or black stripes from the cooking process, and it also has small holes in it. I have heard it described that the flat appearance represents being sinless, the stripes represented our healing through Y'shua's scourging, and the holes were for where Y'shua's hands and feet were pierced. This gives an entirely new depth of meaning when Y'shua broke bread and said, "You must take this and you must now eat, this is My body." (Matthew 26:26) To make this scene even more breath-taking, according to Matthew 26:17, the Seder meal was done during the beginning of the Feast of Unleavened Bread; it would have been Matzah bread that Y'shua handed His Disciples. According to hebrew4christians.com, traditionally the leaven is removed from the home weeks before Pesach (Passover) begins. Y'shua (who will never violate His Scriptures) removed the leaven from His home when He drove out all those who were buying and selling in the Temple in Matthew 21:12-13. Not only was He angry at the deceit and that His people were being taken advantage of, but that sin (leaven) had been brought into His home. In the celebration of the Feast of Unleavened Bread today, ten pieces of leaven are "hidden" throughout the house, and the family of the home would search for it using a candle. The candle could just as easily represent the Word of God which reveals sin. Psalms 119:105 says, "Your Word is a lamp unto my feet and a light unto my path."

 When the family would find the sin, a feather would be used to brush the leaven into a wooden spoon. The family could not stop searching until all of the leaven had been found, no sin could remain in the home which represented the heart. "Search me, O God, and know my heart. Try me and know my thoughts. See if there is any wicked way in me, and lead me in the Way everlasting." (Psalms 139:23-24) Once all of the leaven had been found, they would wrap the spoon, the leaven, and the feather in a white cloth and place it somewhere safe (notice the symbolism to Christ's death and burial?) On the morning of fourteenth day of the Hebrew month of Nissan, the family would gather outside and burn the items for all to see. This was to show that their hearts and home were prepared for Passover. This also "just happens" to be the exact day that Christ would be crucified, removing the leaven from our hearts forever. Praise God!

The next feast was the Feast of First Fruits, where the High Priest would bring a "wave offering" which consisted of the barley harvest. The offering amount was known as an "omer" (or two quarts of barley); and like its name, the "omer" would be waved before the Lord. This feast was also to include a spotless lamb of the first year as a burnt offering. What makes this feast so profound to the followers of Christ is that this Feast is celebrated on the day of His resurrection. This is the reason why Paul referred to Him as the "First Fruits from those who were asleep" in 1 Corinthians 15:20.

Shavuot is a feast that most Christians are familiar with, but we like to refer to it as Pentecost. After the Feast of First Fruits, the children of Israel were to count seven weeks from that day and on the fiftieth day was the Feast of Shavuot. As you read this passage, you'll notice that in verse 21 the Lord says something very interesting, and later on would become very important. It reads, "And you will proclaim on the selfsame day that it is a holy convocation for you, you will do no servile work. It will be a statute forever in all your dwellings throughout your generations." Notice that the Lord made it very clear that they were to never stop practicing this feast throughout their generations. I am sure that this practice as described in Leviticus 21:15-22 didn't make much sense as to why it was so important. For many years in my Christian walk, it didn't make much sense to me either. Yet as we have seen so many times already, Y'shua loves setting up divine appointments. However, to fully grasp this Mo'ed we need to go back to Mount Sinai. When Moses returned from the top of the mountain in Exodus 32, he found that the children of Israel had turned their hearts to a false God made of gold. So Moses divided the people into two groups: those who were for the Lord and those who were against. Moses then ordered the children of Levi to kill those who stood against the Lord throughout the entire camp. In verse 28, we read, "And the children of Levi did according to the word of Moses and there fell of the people that day about three thousand men." Considering that number of people who followed Moses out of Egypt is estimated in the millions, this was a very small number of people who turned away.

    Fast forward to Acts chapter 2, and we see how the Lord will always restore that which was lost. In verse 41, we see the affect of Peter's teaching after being filled with the Holy Spirit. It reads, "Then indeed, those who accepted his message were immersed and there were added on that day about **three thousand lives**." (Emphasis added) How incredible and faithful is our God?! On Mount Sinai, the sins of the people caused Him to lose three thousand souls; on Shavuot (known as the Feast of Weeks in the

Greek) three thousand were added through the outpouring of His Spirit.

The next two feasts are the Day of Memorial (Yom Teruah, Feast of Trumpets) and the Day of Atonement (Yom Kippur). The Day of Memorial is symbolized by the blowing of the Shofars which is a call to repentance. After ten days, Yom Kippur is celebrated and it is known also as the Day of Judgment or the closing of the book. This is certainly not a time to allow our pride and our sin to keep us from repentance.

The final feast during "God's redemptive calendar" is the feast of Sukkot or "Booths." According to William Morford, "This Season came to be called the Tabernacles because the early English translators were from the Latin text and the Latin word for Sukkot, Tabernaculorum, was not translated, but simply transliterated in English." (One New Man Bible p.170) This feast was to remind future Israeli generations of when the Lord brought them out of the land of Egypt, and had them live in temporary dwellings or "booths." Whenever you get a chance, Mark Biltz did an excellent study that shows how Y'shua was born on the first day on the Feast of Sukkot. Aside from the historical evidence, it is so perfect that He would come and "Tabernacle" (which is a temporary dwelling) in flesh with us during the Feast of Tabernacle!

So as you can see, Y'shua has already fulfilled four of the seven feasts and some of them were fulfilled to the hour! Passover (Pesach) was His crucifixion, the Feast of

Unleavened bread (Hag HaMatzot) was His burial, the Feast of First Fruits (Reishit) was His resurrection, and the Feast of Pentecost (Shavuot) was the out pouring of His Holy Spirit. The three remaining feasts: Feast of Trumpets (the rapture), the Feast of Yom Kippur (the Day of Judgment), and the Feast of Tabernacle (the thousand year reign) have still yet to be fulfilled. Once again, the Lord was setting the stage for His Son; just as before, He was doing it in a way that His people would know it was Him.

Chapter 6

The Egypt in our hearts

As you may have already noticed, this book was not intended to be an exhaustive study of the Torah or the Gospel. It was my desire to highlight the consistent trend of the Lord's love towards us, and the methods He uses to draw us ever closer to Himself. With that being said, our search of God's heart picks up in Numbers 13. But, before we continue, there was a very interesting event that took place which I found to be an amazing foreshadowing. In Numbers 11, the children of Israel were complaining because all they had was Manna (Bread of Heaven). In Numbers 11:14-15, Moses responds by saying, "I am not able to carry all these people alone, because they are too heavy for me. And if you deal this way with me, kill me, I pray You, out of hand! If I have found favor in Your sight then do not let me see my wretchedness!" As a result of the people and Moses complaining, the Lord calls for Moses to gather 70 elders, and He would place the same Spirit upon them as was on Moses. The One New Man Bible records that these seventy elders would later become the Sanhedran. So to put it into perspective, the Bread of Heaven was sent to feed the children of Israel, and the Sanhedran was called upon because it was not what the people wanted. When the Bread of Heaven was sent to the House of Bread (Bethlehem) to feed the world; again, this same Sanhedran would be called upon because the bread (Christ) was not what the people were expecting. (John 6:31-36) As I have said before, there are no accidents with God and He is a master at setting the stage for His Glory.

In Numbers 13, we see the Lord calling Israel into a deeper level of faith and trust in Him when He asked them to join the fight. After all of the ups and downs, the plagues, the complaining, the punishments and the rewards, the children of Israel finally stood at the doorstep of the promise land. The Lord told Moses in verse two to "Send for yourself, so they can spy out the land of Canaan, Which I Am giving to the children of Israel." The fact that the Lord said "send for yourself" gives the impression that He wanted to show off His faithfulness to them. The Lord knew what the land held and that it was everything that He promised it would be. However, Moses' response to the Lord's offer was one of fear instead of faith. In verses 17-20, Moses conveys that fear to his spies and (I believe) hinders their ability to see what God had for them. Yes, the fear and unbelief of others can greatly affect our view of God and what He promised. "And Moses sent them to spy out the land of Canaan and said to them, 'Go up here in the south, and go up on the mountain and see the land, what it is and the **people** who live there, whether they are **strong** or **weak**, **few** or **many**. And **what the land is** that they dwell in, whether it is **good** or **bad** and **what cities** there are that they live in, whether **tents** or **strongholds**.

And **what the land is**, whether it is **fat** or **lean**, whether or not there is **wood** in it. And be of good courage and bring of the fruit of the land.' Now the time was the time of the first ripe grapes." (Emphasis added) Can you hear the fear in Moses' voice? Since the day the Lord called Moses to lead His people out of the land of Egypt, He has promised them time and again that it would be a land "flowing with milk and honey." In other words, it was going to be far greater than anything they could have ever imagined! And yet, when the time comes for them to finally take hold of all that God has promised, they focus more on the potential fight that awaits them. Up until this point, the Lord has fought the battles for Israel. They have seen what the Lord can do for them, now He wants them to see what He can do through them. The Lord has just told Moses to spy out the land that He is GIVING them; yet Moses wants the spies to see just how tough it was going to be.

      Whether it is the stock market, coaching sports, choosing a career, or even choosing a spouse, we have a tendency to view life through the eyes of not faith, but risk and reward. What can I gain and how much is it going to cost me? This may seem like a wise approach to life through the eyes of the world, but it will greatly hinder your life of faith. I know the Bible tells us to consider the cost, but it does not tell to retreat from or be consumed by it. Rather, the Bible is telling us to prepare ourselves for the cost, because the reward is great! If you are familiar with this account, you know that Moses' words of fear and uncertainty bore fruit in the hearts of 11 of the 13 spies, and only two were able to see the reward God had promised. Verses 27 and 31 of Numbers 13 pretty much sums up the hearts of the 11. "And they told him and said, 'We came to the land where you sent us and surely it flows with milk and honey, and this is its fruit. **But** the people that live in the land are strong and the cities are walled, very great! And moreover we saw the children of the giant there. Amalek lives in the land of the south and the Hittite, the Jebusite, and the Amorite live in the mountains, and the Canaanites live by the sea and by the Jordan…But the men who went up with him (Caleb) said, We are not able to go up against the people, for they are stronger than we are." That simple three letter word "but" has got to be the most crippling word in the entire English language.

    I wonder how many pastors, teachers, evangelist, singers, writers, and healing ministries failed to come into fruition because of that word. There is so much fear, doubt, frustration, anxiety, and unbelief that the enemy squeezes into that word that boggles my mind. "Lord, I know you have called me to teach Your Word, but I'm not educated. I know You want me to sing the songs You have given me, but no one is going to want to hear them. I know You want me to share my faith, but what if people get offended and hate me? Lord, I know Your Word says to lay hands on the sick and they will recover, but what if it doesn't work?" I am sure there are a million other examples in your own life that you could insert here just as I could, and the ones that I have listed are my own personal "buts." So why is it so hard for us to overcome all of our objections and simply take the land that the Lord has **given** us?

Just like the children of Israel, there are so many examples of His faithfulness that we can look back on and encourage ourselves with. Yet just as they did, we so quickly forget what He has done and we get lost in the little that we ourselves can and can't do. That three letter word changed the course and destiny of an entire nation. In Numbers 14 we read that the children of Israel wept the entire night, and even desired to stone Moses and Aaron for bringing them all this way for "nothing." Now, let's not minimize the difficulty this land appeared to possess. In Numbers 13:33, the word "Nefilim" is used to describe the sons of Anak; and if you remember, this was the same word used to describe the creatures walking upon the earth during the time of Noah.

Goliath was even considered by some to be a Nefilim as well, so this was no small task for the children of Israel **if** they were going to take the land by their own strength. But the key to unravelling this deception was that they were not going to do it alone. I cannot even begin to imagine the hurt and anger that came into the Lord's heart when His people responded this way. After all they had been through, only two (Joshua and Caleb) truly trusted in the Lord's strength and that He was true to His Word. In Numbers 14:6-8 we read, "And Joshua the son of Nun and Caleb the son of Jephunneh, who were of those who spied out the land, tore their clothes, and they spoke to the entire company of the children of Israel saying, 'The land, which we passed through to spy it out, is an exceedingly good land. If the Lord delights in us, then He will bring us into this land and give it to us, a land that flows with milk and honey."

It is absolutely priceless to have "Joshuas and Calebs" in our lives, especially those who are feeling the call into ministry. These are the kind of people that will continue to remind you of the reward when you start getting lost in the risk of God's calling. They are the ones that will hold up your hands to worship when you are weary in battle; they are few and far between. Again, they are priceless. Notice that the spies with the bad report far outnumbered the ones with the good. Negative people are never hard to find, and most of them are the way they are because they have already given up on their own battles. So the fact that you continue to fight only brings about a silent, yet very powerful, conviction. It is so easy for someone to criticize a vision that is not theirs, because what they see is altered by fear rather than focused by faith. Joshua and Caleb remembered all of the acts of power and faithfulness that the Lord had already demonstrated on their behalf. Plus, they remembered that the Lord had told them time and again that He was going to give them the land! So no matter what challenges they saw with their physical eyes, the eyes of their spirits could only see the wealth of the land. Fear is always the easy road. It requires very little effort and it can quickly hinder or even steal all that the Lord has for you. And that loss can have an effect that lasts for generations to come. Even now, many Jews consider the day that the spies brought back a bad report (the 9th of Av) to be a day cursed by God. If you are a student of history, you can easily see why they would believe this. It was on the 9th of the Hebrew month of Av that the First Temple was destroyed by the Babylonians, later the Second Temple was destroyed by the Romans on the same day, and it was this day when the Jews were thrown out of Spain in 1492.

    Just like on Mount Sinai, the Lord tests Moses' heart towards the children of Israel, by telling him once again that He is going to remove them from the face of the earth. In Numbers 14:13-16, we see Moses making a very similar plea to the Lord as he did the first time. However, this time Moses knows the character of God which was revealed to him in Exodus 34. In Numbers 14:17-19, we see a very different description of who the God of Israel is, and notice how similar it is to our current understanding of who Christ is. "And now, I beseech you, let the power of my Lord be great, according as You have spoken saying 'The Lord is patient and of great loving kindness, forgiving iniquity and transgression, and by no means clearing the guilty, visiting the iniquity of the fathers upon the children to the third and fourth generation.' Pardon, I beseech you, the iniquity of this people according to the greatness of Your loving kindness, and as You have forgiven this people from Egypt even until now." When you think about sermons you and I have heard about the God of the "Old Testament," do you ever remember hearing the words "patient, forgiving, and loving kindness?" Now if I were to ask the same question about Christ, 9 times out of 10, the answer would be "yes." And yet, here is the heart of God on display in the Torah long before Y'shua dwelled in flesh with us.

If you remember from earlier, the Hebrew word for "loving kindness" is "Hesed" which is the equivalent of the New Testament "Agape." Even here the Lord is declaring Himself to be a God of unconditional love. In verse 20, the Lord gives Moses His answer, "And the Lord said, 'I have pardon according to your word." This is something else that we are rarely taught about the God of Torah, His desire to pardon sin. Now I know that this is not a cleansing of sin, but a covering like with the burnt offerings. Yet, the fact still remains that the Lord's heart is to forgive His people. Moses did not use some incredible negotiating skills to "sell" God on the idea of keeping the children of Israel alive. The Lord knows the desires of our hearts before we even ask, so I believe the Lord wanted to see if Moses' heart still matched His own towards Israel. Another thing that is often forgotten when we read these accounts in Torah is that God loves His people! If not, why would He be so patient with them? Why would He continue to deliver them and provide for them if He truly hated them? As the account continues in Number 14, we see that the Lord has decided after being tested ten times to not allow the children of Israel to enter into the promise land. Only Caleb, Joshua, and the descendants of Israel younger than 20 years of age will enter in after forty years.

This may sound like a harsh punishment, but even in this declaration we can see God's mercy displayed. Do you remember what Moses said in his description of God in verses 17-19 of this chapter? "The Lord is patient and of great loving kindness, forgiving iniquity and transgression, and by no means clearing the guilty, visiting **the iniquity of the fathers upon the children to the third and forth generation."** So according to the description of Himself that the Lord gave to Moses in Exodus 34, Israel's time in the wilderness should have been much longer. Four generations would have had to live out their lives in the desert before the fifth generation could enter in! And here is the Lord saying that the very next generation will not suffer the full punishment of their fathers, and will enter into the promise land.

      Christmas was my mother's favorite time of year when my brothers and I were growing up, and she just couldn't wait to see our responses to the gifts that she and my dad had purchased. As December 24th grew ever closer, the anticipation would quickly become more than she could bear and she would let us open most of our presents a week early. My dad would get so frustrated that he would have us re-wrap our gifts Christmas Eve, tell us to act surprised, and then he would video tape us opening them. I am pretty sure my grandparents realized rather quickly that we were poor actors. I can see the Lord's heart being much like my mother's when it came to waiting for the children of Israel to enter into the promise land. This was a place much like the Garden of Eden was for Adam: it was a place that the Lord had handcrafted from the foundation of the world just for the ones He loved.

Even now:

At this point, things seem pretty hopeless for the Children of Israel. They have chosen to be led by their fear rather than their faith, they handed back the gift of the promise land in exchange for the Egypt in their hearts, and the Lord has banished them to die in the desert. At this point you are probably wondering how the love of God could be seen in any of this, or even asking the question "why would He want to show them love?" The answer is an incredibly liberating one: our actions do not dictate His love! Sin will always be punished, but until Y'shua returns, love will be waiting on the other side. Numbers chapter 15 gives not only a clear example of this, but also shows a powerful tie to the New Testament, as well. In Numbers 15:37-41 we read, "And the Lord spoke to Moses saying, 'Speak to the children of Israel and bid them to make fringes for themselves in the wings of their garments throughout their generations and that they put upon the fringe of the border a thread of blue, and it will be to you for a fringe, that you may look upon it and remember all the commandments of the Lord and do them, and that you do not seek after you own heart and your own eyes, after which you used to go astray, so you will remember and do all My commandments and be holy to your God. I AM the LORD you God, Who brought you out of the land of Egypt, to be your God: I AM the LORD your God." On its face, this portion of scripture simply seems like the Lord is piling on yet another commandment for the children of Israel to keep up with. In reality, this is the love of God being shown yet again to a people who have turned their backs on Him.

The word "fringe" is "Tzitzit" (Zeet-Zeet) in Hebrew, and since every Hebrew letter and word has a numeric value, the number value for Tzitzit is 600. To create a Tzitzit, you would take 4 strands of string (one of which is blue) and fold them in half to make 8. You would then tie 5 knots in the strings leaving a loop at the top. There are a few more steps that I am leaving out for simplicity's sake, so we don't lose track of the very important numbers being used here. 8 strands (or four folded in half) plus the 5 knots equals 13. Add the 13 to the numeric value of the word Tzitzit (600), and you have a very small token that represents the 613 Levitical Laws (or commandments) of God. This is why to look upon them would remind Israel of God's commandments, but God doesn't stop there. You'll notice that in verse 38, the Lord commands them to place the fringes on the "wings" of their garments. This is referring to the four corners of their prayer shawls or "Tallit (Ta-Leet)." Here is where it starts to get good. The Tallit was also used as a covering or "Hupah" during weddings which the couple would stand under during the ceremony. Since there is a connection here between the Tzitzits and weddings, it is safe to say that these "fringes" were not simply a commandment; they were more like an engagement ring! The children of Israel were to look upon it and remember that their hearts were not their own, or "that you do not seek after your own heart and your own eyes, after which you use to go astray."

Before I got married, my heart (to an extent) was my own to do with as I saw fit. If I want to date, I would date. If I wanted to talk to a pretty girl (and hopefully not fumble over my words in the process) I would go talk to her. However, once I got married and came into a covenant with my wife, my heart was no longer my own. I could not allow it to have the same free reign as it once did, and I was given a visible symbol to remind myself and others of that fact. I said my vows, I was given a ring, and I looked into my wife's beautiful eyes and swore that I would forsake all others so long as we both shall live. Even though this generation of Israel was cut off from the promise land, the Lord is requiring this same level of covenant with them despite their very recent sin. We find out later on in the word that not only would the Tzitzits be a symbol of love, but it would proclaim who Christ was and bring healing!

In Malachi 3:20 (the chapter and verse numbers may be different in different translations) we read, "But to you who revere My Name, the Sun of Acts of Loving

Kindness (Hesed) will rise with healing in His wings and you will go out to and prosper like fattening calves in the stalls." Notice that this passage says that there will be healing in His wings, and we know from earlier that this is referring to Y'shua Tallit. In Luke 8:43-48, we read, "And a woman who was in a flow of blood for twelve years, who having spent her whole living on doctors was not able to be healed by anyone, when she came up behind she touched the **fringe** of His prayer shawl and immediately her flow of blood was stopped. Then Y'shua said, 'Who is the one who touched Me?' But all denied, Peter said, 'Master, the crowds are choking You and pressing in.' And Y'shua said, 'Someone touched Me. For I know power has come out from Me.' And when the woman saw that she did not escape notice, she came trembling and as she fell before Him she reported before all of the people what the reason was she touched Him and as she spoke she was healed immediately. And He said to her, 'Daughter, your faith has saved you. You must continually go in peace."

    Now, many translations will say that she grabbed the "hem" of His garment; but during that time, it was not customary to hem garments. Plus, this woman would have known the practice/purpose of the Tzitzits as well as the prophecy of Malachi, so what she was reaching for was very specific and powerful. If that weren't enough, this practice was later repeated and many more people were healed. In Mark 6:53-56 we read, "Then after they crossed to the shore they came into Gennesaret and entered the harbor. And when they came off of the boat, immediately recognizing Him they were running about that whole region, and they began to bring up their mattresses those who had evil wherever they heard that He was. And whenever He went in villages or in cities or in hamlets, they placed the sick in the markets and were begging Him that they could just **touch the fringe of His prayer shawl**: and as many as were touching it were being delivered. (Emphasis added)" I have to admit, once I learned about this incredible act of love, covenant, and power that the Lord gave/showed His people, I began wearing Tzitzits myself! Here we have the children of Israel in freshly committed sin, and the Lord decides that now is the time to enter into this covenant with them. It would be like going to someone who just betrayed your love and asking them to marry you. Yet that is exactly what the Lord was doing with Israel in the wilderness. He was once again taking a rebellious people and setting them apart for Himself; and by telling Israel to keep this practice throughout their generations, He was preparing the day of one faithful woman's healing all the way back in Numbers. His love stretches from everlasting to everlasting!

Whom I love, I have chosen:

As our journey through Numbers continues, we find Moses and Aaron's authority being challenged once again. However, this time it is coming from a very unlikely source in that the two hundred and fifty sons of Levi are the ones bringing the charge against them. To make matters worse, Kohath, Dathan, and Abiram are leading them and these men are known to be "men of renown" according to Numbers 16:2. To summarize, these men have convinced two hundred and fifty of their fellow Levites that Moses and Aaron were at fault for keeping the children of Israel out of the Promise Land. They have also said that Moses and Aaron did this so they could remain in charge over the multitude. Yet, Moses' response showed the level of relationship that he had with the Lord. Moses could have easily reminded them of all the times they turned their back on God, and how many times he had to plead with the Lord not to destroy them. Instead, Moses asked them why being set apart from the multitude by God to serve in the temple wasn't enough for them. Then he challenges them on the depth of their relationship with God through worship.

    This meant so much to me because Moses didn't feel the need to defend himself. He wasn't insecure in his calling nor was he going to go out of his way to prove his calling. Essentially, Moses told them to come to the Lord with him and see who God chooses. Numbers 16:16-22 says, "And Moses said to Korah, 'You and all your company be before the Lord: you and they and Aaron, tomorrow. And every man take his fire-pan before the Lord, two hundred fifty fire-pans; you also and Aaron, each of you his fire-pan.' And each man took his fire-pan and put fire in it and laid incense on it, and stood at the door of the Tent of Meeting with Moses and Aaron. And Korah gathered the entire congregation against them at the door of the Tent of Meeting: and the glory of the Lord appeared to the whole congregation. And the Lord spoke to Moses and to Aaron saying, 'Separate yourselves from among this congregation, so I can consume them in a moment.' And they fell upon their faces and said, 'O God, the God of the spirits of flesh, will one man sin and will You be angry with the whole congregation?"

You may be wondering where the worship is in this passage, it is the burning of the incense. Just like the smoke from a burnt offering was considered an act of worship and a sweet savor to the Lord (Genesis 8:21), so was the burning of incense like praise being lifted before the Lord. The Lord later tells Moses and the congregation to separate themselves from Korah, Dathan, and Abiram; the three men were swallowed up by the earth along with all of their possessions. Moses knew the love that the Lord had for him, so he knew what God's answer was going to be. This trust in the Lord's love came from time spent with Him, much like the love between a married couple. If a husband or a wife do not spend much time together or even really know each other's hearts, then the fear of that love failing is hard to fight off. But if there has been time spent cultivating and nurturing that relationship, then the question of whether or not the other still loves them is easily answered.

I can remember so many times in the past feeling like I needed to defend or convince others of the calling that the Lord had placed in my life. Feelings of insecurity and doubt became very difficult to overcome and that same insecurity would spill over into how I shared my faith. Any time my faith was challenged by someone who didn't believe or was of another faith, I felt that it was my duty to make them understand and accept the way I saw the Lord through scripture. When I would "lose" this challenge, I would leave feeling frustrated and would sometimes begin questioning what I believed to be true about the Word. Slowly over time, the Lord began to release me from this burden that I had placed upon myself. Especially when I began to see how Y'shua didn't feel the need to defend Himself either.

He knew His Father's heart towards Him, and it was the Lord's job to show the world who Christ was whether they received Him or not. You'll notice that Christ never begged anyone to believe in Him, and He even allowed people to leave a conversation with Him still not believing! However, when the challenges came, the Lord defended His own. That is why Y'shua said in John 5:19-20, "Most assuredly I say to you, the Son is not able to do anything by Himself except what He would see the Father doing; for whatever that One would do, then the Son likewise does these things. **For the Father loves the Son** and shows Him everything that He does and greater works than these will He show to Him, so that you would be amazed." If we are doing what the Lord has called us to do, then He is the one who will qualify us, defend us to others, and show us what He wants us to do simply because He loves us.

More than water:

I have found that my heart's truest desires, beliefs, and intentions are revealed during times of lacking or hardship. And as much as I hate these times, it challenges me to be the fruit inspector of my faith. For the sake of being transparent, I'll admit that I don't always seem very "Christian" during those times and I have made some pretty foolish accusations of the Lord. So when I read about the seemingly constant swaying of faith to doubt by the children of Israel, I am quickly reminded of my own struggles and of Christ' incredible patience with me. I have also found that when I finally turn to Him during these times, He shows Himself mighty in a whole new way. We see this in Numbers 20:6-8, "Then Moses and Aaron went from the presence of the assembly to the door of the Tent of Meeting, and they fell upon their faces and the glory of the Lord appeared to them. And the Lord spoke to Moses saying, 'Take the staff and gather the assembly together, you and Aaron your brother, and speak to the rock before their eyes and it will give forth its water and you will bring water out of the rock to them: so you will give the congregation and the beast their drink." The key point to this scripture it that the Lord told Moses to "speak to the rock" and an abundance of water would flow from it. If you remember in Exodus 17:6 we read, "Behold, I shall stand in front of you there on the rock in Horeb and you will strike the rock, and there water will come out of it, so the people can drink." The wording here is so powerful because the Lord said "I shall stand in front of you on the rock...," so we have the picture of Christ being lifted up, struck, and water flowing. Even more incredible is the Strong's definition (H5553) for the word "rock" in this scripture means "a cliff." Now we have the picture of Y'shua on top of a cliff or mount while He is being struck!

    As we continue reading in Numbers 20, we find that Moses struck the rock twice instead of speaking to it as the Lord commanded and he was greatly punished for it. In Numbers 20:12 we read, "And the Lord spoke to Moses and Aaron, 'Because you did not believe Me, to sanctify Me in the eyes of the children of Israel, therefore you will not bring this congregation into the land which I have given them." This may seem rather harsh of the Lord until you realize what He was trying to do. Notice that He said this act of speaking to the rock (or cliff) would "sanctify (to make Holy or Proclaim) Me in the eyes of the children of Israel..." The Lord not only wanted to set the stage once again for Y'shua for a future event to declare who He was, but He wanted to show Israel yet another level of the kind of relationship they could have with Him. A glimpse, if you will, into the kind of relationship we have with Him now. In John 19:33-34, we see the stage that the Lord was trying to set in Numbers 20. It reads, "...and when they came to Y'shua, as they saw that He was already dead, they did not break His legs, but one of the soldiers pierced His side with his spear and immediately blood and water came out." The Rock of our Salvation was lifted up on a mount, struck, and water flowed from Him. Since our Rock has been stricken once and for all for us, then we only need to speak to Him and the cleansing water of His spirit and His provision will wash over us. The Lord wanted the children of Israel to see that they didn't have to strive to receive anything from Him, the price had already been paid (figuratively) in Exodus and has been paid for us all in the Gospels. Christ is the river of living water the psalmist said for us to be planted by (Psalms 1:3), He is the "way in the wilderness and rivers in the desert" (Isaiah 43:19). The Lord is showing us so much in these two accounts of Moses and the rock, it was literally the "Good News" being declared in Exodus and Numbers. We cannot continue to love the Lord, and at the same time, feel like we have to demand or fight Him for our needs. The Bible says that when we turn away from Him after tasting of His goodness, we crucify the Son of God anew and openly shame Him (Hebrews 6:6)...we strike the Rock again in front of the world. He is not withholding one good thing from us, the Rock has already been struck, all we have to do is speak to the Rock in faith and the supply for our physical and spiritual needs will flow from Him in abundance.

The way I see you:

      In our journey through Exodus and Numbers so far, it is easy to pick up on the pattern of Israel's unfaithfulness. They complain, the Lord performs a mighty work, they repent, they rejoice, and they complain again. Even though it is easy to criticize their lack of faith, I know that there is an area in all of our lives where we continually fall short. To make matters worse, the moment we fall, our enemy is ever ready to tell us we are not worthy of forgiveness. We are told that the Lord could not possibly want us back, and that He only sees us as failures. The part of us not being worthy of His forgiveness is more than accurate, but the enemy always tries to deceive with partial truths. The Lord is ready to receive us back with open arms and He is right there the moment we cry out. We are promised this in 1 John 1:9 which says, "If we confess our sins, He is faithful and righteous, so that He would forgive our sins and He would cleanse us from all unrighteousness." In Number 22-24, we get the privilege of not only seeing how the Lord views the children of Israel, but us as well.

      We start with Balak who is the King of the Moabites. He has seen Israel's large numbers as well as their victories against the Amorites, and he was greatly afraid that he and his kingdom would be consumed as well. So Balak seeks out Balaam (who is a man of God) to speak a curse against the children of Israel. To do this, Balak sends elders with rewards to Balaam in hopes of convincing him. When Balaam hears Balak's request, he asks the elders to stay the night so he could seek the Lord on the issue. During Balaam's prayer time, the Lord reveals to Balaam that Israel is His people and he is not to do what the king has requested. When Balak heard the news of Balaam's response, he sent princes and even greater rewards hoping to sway Balaam's heart. Now, the Lord's anger is kindled against Balaam at this point, because he is seeking the Lord for an answer that has already been given to him. The Lord tells Balaam to go with the princes; and while traveling to Balak, the Lord uses Balaam's donkey to warn him one last time not to speak against the Lord's chosen people. Even now, we see the Lord's mercy towards Balaam.

In Number 22:31-33 we read, "Then the Lord opened Balaam's eyes and he saw the angel of the Lord standing in the way, and his sword drawn in his hand: and he bowed down his head and fell on his face. And the angel of the Lord said to him, 'Why have you hit your donkey these three times? Look, I purposely came out to stop you because your way is perverse before me. And the donkey saw me, and turned from me these three times: if it had not turned from me, surely now I would have slain you and saved it alive." The Lord then tells Balaam to go to Balak and speak the words that He would give him. When Balaam arrives, Balak tries to convince Balaam two more times to curse Israel and he even offers seven burnt offerings to try and sway God's heart as well! On his third and final attempt, Balak takes Balaam up to a high place so he can see the children of Israel with his own eyes. Only this time, Balaam seeks the Lord's heart towards Israel instead of His enchantments. All this brings us to yet another stunning revelation about God's heart towards His people.

Number 23:18-22 we read, "And he took up his parable, and said, 'Rise up, Balak, and hear! Listen to me, you son of Zippor: God is not a man that He should lie, nor the son of man, that He should be sorry. Has He said and will He not do it? Or has He spoken and will He not make it good? Look, I have taken the message to bless. And he has blessed and I cannot reverse it. He has not beheld iniquity in Jacob, **nor has He seen evil deeds in Israel**. The Lord God is with him and the shout of a king is among them. God Who brought them out of Egypt has as it were the strength of a buffalo (Emphasis added)." I cannot even begin to wrap my brain around this revelation of how the Lord sees Israel! How on earth after everything Israel has done, can the Lord place in a man's heart that He has not seen any evil deeds in Israel? If you are like me, you don't have to dig deep in your memory bank to remember something "evil" or sinful that you have done. Yet when we repent, this is exactly how He sees us. Once again, the Lord wanted Israel to know how they look through His eyes. They are His and He loves them, He defends them, He fights for them, He blesses those who bless them, and He curses those who curse them. How comforting it is to know that God's love towards us is not dependent on us?! This of course is not a license to sin, but the knowledge that His view of us will not change. Even if there is sin in our lives that is hindering our walk with Him, it is His loving kindness (His Hesed) that brings us to repentance. Not only that, but the Lord had orchestrated this event and lead them to the Moabites to reveal His heart to His people. If we were to go back to Numbers chapters 20-21, you would see that the king of Edom, the king of the Canaanites, and the king of the Amorites all denied Israel entry into their lands. The Lord was intentionally shutting doors so that Israel would be led straight to Balaam's revelation of who they are. If that wasn't enough, this entire incident between Balak and Balaam would have to have been made known to Moses, or he would not have written it down in God's word.

This is a very power declaration that I recommend you make over yourself when the enemy brings God's love for you into question. Try personalizing it to really drive home the point that you are loved and cared for. For example, "Rise up, (your name), and hear! Listen to me, you son (or daughter) of Majesty: God is not a man that he should lie, nor the son of man, that He should be sorry. Has He said and will He not do it? Or has He spoken and will He not make it good? Look, the Lord has taken this message to bless me. And He has blessed and the enemy cannot reverse it! He has not beheld iniquity in me, nor has He seen evil deeds in my walk (after you have repented). The Lord my God is with me and the shout of the King of Kings in among my home. God Who has brought me out of (list past bondage that He has freed you from) has as it were the strength of a buffalo." God's love for us is so often the first area that the enemy attacks when we go through trials and tribulations. If he can get us to question God's love, then we will soon doubt His faithfulness and His Word. As a result, we will fall into the same trap that Israel did time and again, by blaming the One Who alone can save us.

On a side note, I can't help but admire Balaam's statement in this account and his willingness to turn down wealth and promotion to honor the Lord. How many times are we faced with the decision of going against what we know honors the Lord, and possibly missing out on more money or even losing our jobs. Going back to Numbers 22:18, Balaam makes a stand that came at a perfect time for me when I was faced with a similar decision; "And Balaam answered and said to the servants of Balak, 'If Balak would give me his house full of silver and gold, I cannot go beyond the word of the Lord my God, to do less or more." I heard a friend say that when we are more concerned about provision than the Lord's leading, it is because we have taken on an orphan's mindset. An orphan has to hoard and constantly seek out provision, because they have no one to care for them. This is not who we are. We are joint heirs with Christ who holds all of the wealth and riches of this world in his hands.

Chapter 7

Prepare to receive

    I have heard it said that "there is no such thing as an atheist in a fox hole (author unknown);" and although there is a level of humor in this state, there is also a very powerful underlining truth. There is something about overcoming in battle that brings people closer to each other and to the Lord. For a brief time, I was on a S.W.A.T. team before having to move to another department due to financial hardship. I trained for five months so I could endure a two day tryout that was both physically and mentally demanding. Out of the sixteen officers that tried out for the team, I was one of eight who was able to make it to the end. Most of us, myself included, lost 10lbs in those two grueling days and I had never been more exhausted in my entire life. However, as my seven teammates and I stood there at the end of the covered in water, sweat, snot, and tear gas (CS), the Captain over the tryout asked us if we felt like we had accomplished anything. After answering with an out of breath "yes sir," he said the words we had fought so hard to hear: "Well, congratulations you're S.W.A.T." We had been tested by fire and we came out on top. However, I would not have come close to accomplishing this task if I did not prepare. I had to train myself for the mental and physical demands that were about to be placed upon me so I could endure to the end. As we enter into the book of Deuteronomy, we see this same dynamic begin to take place between the Lord and Israel. Moses has been told by the Lord that their time in the wilderness is about to come to an end. In fact, the entire book of Deuteronomy covers the last two months before the children of Israel would enter into the promise land. This time of preparation was so important to the Lord, because He didn't just want the people to get the land; He wanted them to be able to keep it.

Don't forget me:

      The wait is finally over, and the generation that the Lord has risen up from among the children of Israel is about to enter the Land of Promise. So much has been lost and learned during the forty years in the wilderness, and now the Lord wants His people to be up for the challenge. Not only that, but He is also now dealing with a generation that grew up outside of Egypt. Many of them did not witness the Lord's mighty miracles in the plagues, or see Him descend onto the top of Mount Sinai in a cloud of fire. So essentially, He has to teach them anew as to Who He is and how He loves them. To do this, He starts by reminding them of all that He has done. The Lord tells Moses to remind the people of the journey they took to get to where they are now. He reminds the people of the faithfulness of His leading and all of the battles that He helped them win. He tells them of the Amorites, of Heshbon, and of Bashan. This has been a common practice of the Lord to remind His people to what He has done; for example, you'll notice that the Lord has said time and again "I am the Lord your God who brought you out of the land of Egypt." He spends the first three chapters reminding them of their victories, but He also reminds them of the 9th of Av when the ten spies brought back the bad report. I love the way Moses words it in Deuteronomy 4:32-35, "For ask now of the days that are past, which were before you, since the day that God created man on the earth, and ask from the one side of heaven to the other, whether there has been any such thing as this great thing is, or has been heard like it? Did a people ever hear the voice of God speaking out of the midst of the fire, as you have heard, and live? Or has God attempted to take for Himself a nation from the midst of another nation, by temptations, by signs, by wonders, by war, by the mighty hand, by an outstretched arm, and by the terrors, according to all that the Lord your God did for you in Egypt before your eyes? It was shown to you so that you would know that the Lord, He is God."

Moses is asking the children of Israel a very simple question here: "Who else has God blessed like the way He has blessed you?" We can ask ourselves that very same question. I know that many people have been healed and provided for, but what makes your own personal testimony of His faithfulness unique is how it was done in a way that you knew in your heart it was Him and He did it just for you. Even though we hear about so many miracles all around us, we don't think that the Lord did it simply because that is what He does. We have this overwhelming sense inside that He did it just for us. Yet as I have said before, the enemy always attacks God's faithfulness to us whenever we go through hardship. The Lord knows this and that is why He is getting Israel ready now before they even enter in. Fear, doubt, and unbelief always comes rushing in the moment we begin to question God's love for us. Our greatest weapon to combat this is the word of our testimony. We have to stir our hearts and our spirits with examples of how He has brought us through in the past. If you remember when Moses and the children of Israel were building the Ark of the Covenant: they placed in it the Ten Commandments, ashes of a red heifer, Aaron's rod that bloomed, and a bowl of manna. All of these were to be reminders of Him!

The Ten Commandments were to remind the people how to avoid sin, the ashes of a red heifer was to remind them of His covenant with them, Aaron's rod that bloom was to remind them that their leaders were specifically chosen by God, and the bowl of manna was to reminded them that He alone is there provision and sustainer. This is why it is so important to keep a journal of all the hardships Y'shua has brought you through, and all of the miracles He has performed in your life. By doing so, you are creating your own "Ark of the Covenant" that will strengthen your faith whenever you begin to waver.

      Isn't it amazing that the foundation the Lord wanted to lay in the children of Israel's hearts was the memory of His love for them? This is what everything is built upon; the commandments, the feasts, clean and unclean, holy and unholy, it is all rooted and grounded in the knowledge of His relentless love. Even the incredible hardships and evil the children of Israel had to endure, the Lord was using it and turning it for their good. If we go back to Deuteronomy 4:20, we see Moses make a statement that is almost beyond comprehension. It reads, "But the Lord has taken you and brought you forth out of the iron furnace, out of Egypt, to be to Him a people of inheritance, as you are this day." Four hundred and thirty years of slavery that the enemy was using to mercilessly oppress God's people, the Lord was using to prepare a nation for Himself. What if the "impossible" circumstance that you are going through right now is not God being indifferent to your situation, but rather, He is turning it for your good so you could obtain and sustain all that He has for you? God is assuring Israel (and us) that the battles they are about to face belong to Him, but next He must prepare for the spiritual battles that await them as well.

A hedge around their hearts:

If there has ever been an area the enemy has "duped" the modern day church, it would be in the area of spiritual warfare. For some of you, the very thought causes you to picture people rolling on the ground, picking up snakes, and throwing "Holy Water" everywhere. Needless to say, this is one of many biblical principles that a have been taken to the extreme by some churches. However, this by no means diminishes its importance in our Christian walk and our day to day lives. We have a tendency to live like the spiritual realm is a fantasy that makes for really good movie plots. Yet, as we get into Deuteronomy 6 we see that the Lord through Moses is trying to prepare the children of Israel for more than one battle field. The Lord knows the hearts of His people and how they have fallen away before. The golden calf, leaders within Israel's camp trying to rise up against Moses and Aaron, as well as all of those men who were seduced by the Moabite women. Now, the children of Israel are moving into enemy occupied territory and there are demons there that do not wish to be dethroned. Deuteronomy 6:1-9 pretty much lays out the plan on how Israel will be able to withstand the spiritual attacks of the enemy.

"Now this is the commandment – the statutes and the rules – that the Lord your God commanded me to teach you, that you may do them in the land to which you are going over, to possess it, that you may fear the Lord your God, you and your son and your son's son, by keeping all His statutes and His commandments, which I command you, all the days of your life, and that your days may be long. Hear therefore, O Israel, and be careful to do them, that it may go well with you, and that you may multiply greatly, as the Lord, the God of your fathers, has promised you, in a land flowing with milk and honey. Hear, O Israel: The Lord our God, the Lord is One. You shall love the Lord with all your heart and with all your soul and with all you might. And these words that I command you today shall be on your heart. You shall teach them diligently to your children, and shall talk of them when you sit in your house, and when you walk by the way, and when you lie down, and when you rise. You shall bind them as a sign on your hand, and they shall be as frontlets between your eyes. You shall write them on the door post of your house and your gate. (The Study Bible)" So what is the plan? Immerse yourself in the Word of God constantly. In the first two verses, we see that the Lord is wanting this to be a generational blessing and that their days in the land may be long. The Lord doesn't just want them to receive the blessing; He wants them to be able to sustain it. God doesn't bless us haphazardly; they are intentional and they are ones that He has grown us towards because He loves us. It would be like handing your child the keys to a brand new car having never taught them how to drive. Let them get into an accident, or receive their first speeding ticket due to a lack of knowledge, and suddenly that gift feels more like a curse.

Having a strong memory and understanding of the Word doesn't just help to do what's right, but it helps us to recognize when something is wrong. In Law Enforcement, I saw fake IDs and fake currency all the time and I have been asked how we are able to spot a counterfeit so quickly. Even though criminals create thousands of new twists in driver's licenses and US currency, we keep our training very simple. We only study the real thing. Once you have a working knowledge of what the real thing looks like, the fakes stick out like a sore thumb. The same holds true with the Word of God, so it is no wonder that the Lord reminds them of the commandments He gave them at Mount Sinai.

No compromises:

The next step in preparing the children of Israel for the Promise Land is what to do with conquered enemies. This is another area that can cause people to question that the Lord has always been a God of love. In Deuteronomy 7:1-2 we read, "When the Lord your God brings you into the land where you are going to possess it and has cast out many nations before you, the Hittite, the Gergashite, the Amorite, the Canaanite, the Perizzite, the Hivite, and the Jebusite, seven nations greater and mightier than you, and when the Lord your God delivers them from before you and you strike them, utterly destroying them, you will make no covenant with them or show them favor." So basically, the Lord is telling the Israelites that when He helps them conquer their enemies, completely wipe them out. He goes on to say in verse five, "But this is how you will deal with them: you will destroy their altars, break down their images, cut down their groves, and burn their graven images with fire." The Lord is warning them that if they allow just a few of them to live, if they marry their daughters and give their daughter's over for marriage, they will be deceived into following false gods and will turn away from the Lord. Sin cannot be allowed to remain no matter how small or innocent it may seem. One of the enemy's greatest tricks is to present himself as weak and harmless, and that there are "big sins" and then there are "little harmless sins." It is like a recovering alcoholic leaving just a few beers in his refrigerator; we know that the taste of those two beers will inspire him/her to buy more. That is what makes the "little sins" so dangerous: their gain appears to far outweigh the risks. Yet we fail to realize that each sin is just a small step off of the path of holiness. The next thing you know, you wake up and realize that you are saying and doing things you never thought you would.

    We need to take this "Promise Land" approach to sin in our own lives, and I know this can be a difficult and sometimes painful process. The best analogy when it comes to the Lord removing sin from our lives is going into surgery to have a cancerous tumor removed. The doctor must "hurt" you in order to get to what is killing you, and the wound he makes when he cuts open your flesh with a knife will leave a scar. Yet, have you ever noticed that a cancer survivor rarely complains about the "harm" the doctor causes, but instead they tell everyone of what the doctor delivered them from. Not to mention, you will never hear the doctor say, "We left a little of the cancer in you, but you should be alright. It's just a little bit." So why do we not do the same when it comes to the Lord saving us from the sin in our lives? The enemy tries to convince us that God's process will be more painful than the effect of the sin. It isn't until we have been freed from the bondage of sin that we truly realize just how much it was killing us. There is more to the Lord's plan here than just the children of Israel being "good" and His other motive once again is something you may not hear taught very often. In verses 6-9 we read, "For you are a holy people to the Lord your God. The Lord your God has chosen you to be special people for Himself, above all the people that are on the face of the earth.

The Lord did not set His love upon you, nor choose you because you were more in number than any people, for you were the fewest of all people, but because the Lord loved you and because He would keep the oath which He had sworn to your fathers, the Lord has brought you out with a mighty hand and redeemed you from the house of bondage, from the hand of Pharaoh king of Egypt. Know therefore that the Lord is your God! He is God, the Faithful God Who keeps covenant and loving kindness with those who love Him and keep His commandments, to a thousand generations." He is telling them these things because He loves them and He wants them all to Himself!

Nothing is more wonderful than to be in a relationship or marriage where you feel both needed and wanted. So the Lord is not telling Israel to wipe everyone out because He is a blood thirsty God, but because He knows that these people will be used by the enemy to lead what He loves away from Him. Just as a toxic relationship must be cut off completely, so to must the sin in our lives be shown no mercy. Or else we will be deceived by the memories of the "good times" and will be lead right back into bondage. At the end of the day, His desire for us to be pure and holy is because He loves us more than anything. Even the way He plans on having them enter into the Promise Land screams of His love for them. You'll notice back in verse one that the wording is "When the Lord your God brings you into the land..." He isn't driving them, ordering them, or even commanding them, He is bringing them into the land as if He is welcoming them into a place that was already His. When I read this, I can picture a groom carrying his bride across the threshold of the doorway to their new lives together.

It is also important to note the hatred that the Lord has towards idols and He wants them destroyed by fire. He doesn't say out it in the shed or put them in the attic; He desires that our idols be put into a state where they can never ensnare us again. Now, when we think of idols, we often picture a statue of some animal or pagan god that people worship and such was the case during this time. However, our idols today have become much harder to identify and even more difficult to destroy. So what does a modern day idol look like? It is anything that consumes your time and money more than the Lord. I love the way the Amplified Bible words it in Matthew 6:21, "….for where your treasure is, there your heart [your wishes, your desires; that on which your life centers] will be also." The key phrase in that translation is "that on which your life centers." So ask yourself, "What does my life center around?" Is it work, a relationship, a title or maybe a hobby? I am going to call myself out and say that for a long time my idol was video games; sadly, I don't mean when I was a kid. I used to justify that it was my way to unwind from a hard day, my escape, my….drug? Oops, sorry fellow gamers, but this too can become an addiction, and very much so, an idol. It sickens me to think of the years (not just hours) of my life that I wasted on something that bore absolutely no fruit, and left me with nothing to show for my "accomplishments."

    A good way to tell if something has become an idol is what I like to call the "quitting test." Try giving that one thing up for a month and see how hard it is to not want to go back to it. The harder the temptation is to go back, the greater the idol and the hold that it has on your heart. Every time I have attempted to be a "casual gamer," I have ended up putting 40 hours a week into my little past time. Then I would make the argument that I just don't have the "time" to spend time with the Lord or read his Word. Idols consume time that is both limited and on loan to us by God Himself. We have been placed on this earth during this specific time in eternity for a very specific purpose. The Lord has crafted both time and history, preparing the world for your arrival so you would have the most potential to create the greatest impact. So do not allow your heart to be distracted by idols that would steal you time and your ministry, destroy them with the same passion and hatred that the Lord has for them. You may not yet realize how valuable you are to the advancement of the Lord's kingdom, but rest assured: you enemy does. And he will stop at nothing to pull you away from the purpose the Lord has for your life.

The Lord's heart in the Shemitah:

If you are familiar with the writings of Johnathan Cahn, then you may have heard of his book titled *"The Mystery of the Shemitah."* In his book, Pastor Cahn talks about the how the Lord has blessed the nation that honors the seventh year rest and the financial hardship that that befalls those who don't. Pastor Cahn also points out how all of the financial collapses that America has had to endure since the 1940s have fallen on a Shemitah year. We find the commandment of the Shemitah year by the Lord in Deuteronomy 15, and we can see why this time is so important to Him. First off, the word "Shemitah" means a release from labor and debts (Chabad.org). The Lord told the children of Israel to forgive each other's debt; and to release each other from servitude to repay a debt every seven years. Can you imagine if you house, car, and credit card debt was wiped clean every seven years? But the Lord took this commandment ever further. In chapter 15:7 we read, "If there is a poor man with you of your brothers within any of your gates in your land which the Lord your God gives you, you will not harden your heart or shut your hand from your poor brother, but you will open your hand wide to him and will surely lend him sufficient for his need, for that which he lacks." This year of released financial blessings was the Lord giving seeds to the sower, so they could invest into those in need and receive a double blessing. One for obeying the Shemitah and one for giving generously to the poor. In verse 10 of the same chapter we read, "You will surely give to him and your heart will not be grieved when you give to him. Because of this, the Lord your God will bless you in all your works and in all that you put your hand to."

    I myself have been guilty of being hesitant to give to a poor person out of fear of what they may use it for. What if I give then money and they spend it on drugs or alcohol? You'll notice that the Lord does not tell us to determine the intensions of the poor before giving to them. He simply says give and He will do the rest. A person may be able to escape our presence, but they cannot escape our prayers. The next time you give, pray that you have seeded into that person's salvation and long term provision.

Also, if a fellow Hebrew was sold to them as a servant, they were to be set free in the Shemitah year as well and they were not to be released empty handed. In Deuteronomy 15:13-14 we read, "And when you send him out free from you, you will not let him go empty. You will furnish him liberally from your flock, from your threshing floor, and from your wine press. You will give to him from that with which the Lord your God has blessed you." What an amazing way to live and what a testimony of God's love to each other. Yet, there is an even more powerful message being conveyed to the children of Israel. This is not just a simple act of graciousness towards others, but a reenactment of what the Lord has done for them. If you remember in Exodus 11:2-3 we read, "Speak now in the ears of the people, let each man ask from his neighbor, and each woman from her neighbor, jewels of silver, and jewels of gold. And the Lord gave the people favor in the sight of the Egyptians. Moreover, the man Moses was very great in the land of Egypt, in the sight of Pharaoh's servants and in the sight of the people." The Lord wanted His people to demonstrate the same love and mercy that He showed them, so the children of Israel would be blessed and others would be reminded of the faithfulness of their God. This is also the portion of scripture where we see the process of becoming a "bond servant." In

Deuteronomy 15:16-17 we read, "And it will be, if he says to you, I shall not go away from you, because he loves you and your house, because he is well with you, then you will take an awl and thrust it through his ear to the door and he will be your servant forever." It is this process that made Paul's description of himself in Romans 1:1 so deep, when he said that he was a "bond servant of Messiah Y'shua." He was declaring that he was a slave to sin with a debt he could never repay, Christ redeemed his debt and gave Him the option to leave, and because of His love Paul chose to remain a willing servant. In a spiritual sense, Paul is declaring that he has nailed his own ear to the cross and will remains Christ's servant forever. This is our proclamation to the world as to why we are "followers of the Way." It amazes me how we have taken such a simple message and made it so complex. We have created formulas, programs, self-helps, and catch phrases to try and convince ourselves that we are right. To make matters worse, we believe that because we have accomplished so much in these behavior modifications (not true deliverance) that somehow God owes us. When in reality all the Lord is telling us back in Deuteronomy is that He will bless those who mimic the love He has already demonstrated. The heart of the Shemitah is deliverance and redemption, which is the prefect reflection of the heart of the One Who created it.

Chapter 8

A God we can touch

As the Torah comes to a conclusion, we see Moses giving the children of Israel a final warning not to turn away from the commandments of the Lord. Moses also lays his hands on Joshua and he is filled with both the spirit and the wisdom to lead the people into the Promise Land. Yet, it is how the Lord described His relationship with Moses that shows the love He had for him. In Deuteronomy 34:10 we read, "And in Israel there has not risen a prophet like Moses, whom the Lord knew face to face." What a beautiful description of the kind of relationship they had. The attitude between the two of them was not one of "Master and servant," but of close friends who were able to look each other in the eye. Now that the Lord had given the children of Israel His commandments, it was time for them to live it out. As you may know, as you continue reading the accounts of Israel, there were many times where they would succeed and many times where they would turn away and fail. Yet, there was this lingering promise that kept reoccurring throughout the Old Testament. It gave the Word the feel as if history was slowly building to a fixed point in time, and we see yet another hint of it in Deuteronomy 18:15. "The Lord your God will rise up for you a prophet (Y'shua) like me from among you, of your brothers. You will listen to Him..." From Genesis to Deuteronomy, the Lord has laid the foundation for His Word and the revelation of His true heart towards us. As we have seen already, God's love towards us has been evident from the very beginning. A love that can be so easily short changed simply from a lack of knowledge and a skewed view of the Word. Now as we transition into the Gospel, my hope is to connect it to the Torah in a way that will not only show a greater depth to His love, but also a better understanding as to why some seemingly small things that the Lord did meant so much to so many.

A message to His own:

Before we dive into the book of Matthew, it is important to note exactly who the Gospel was originally written for so we can better understand His message. First, according to the templemount.org there was a four hundred year period between the book of 2 Chronicles (last written book of the Old Testament) and the book of Matthew. This period of time was spoken about in Amos 8:11-12, "Behold, the days are coming with Adonai the Lord, that I shall send a famine in the land, not a famine of bread nor a thirst for water, but of hearing the words of the Lord and they will wander from sea to sea and from the north even to the east. They will run to and fro to seek the word of the Lord and will not find it." The time that Christ is stepping into is one ruled by a very pagan Roman Empire, Hellenist Jews that have been seduced by Greek Mythology are prevalent, and His people are bogged down by what is known as "fence laws." "Fence Laws" were oral rules (or laws) placed on top of the Torah commandments, in hopes of preventing the Jewish people from violating God's Word. The additional laws that were thought to help keep people in step with the Torah, ended up resulting in bondage, confusion, and deception. A good example of this can be found back in Genesis with Adam and Eve. In Genesis 2:15 we read, "And the Lord God took the man and put him in the Garden of Eden to till it and keep it. And the Lord God commanded man saying, 'You may freely eat of every tree of the garden, but you will not eat of the tree of the knowledge of good and bad, for in the day that you eat of it you will surely die."

Notice that the Lord's commandment was not to eat the fruit; if you look at Eve's response to Satan's temptation, the "fence law" becomes pretty easy to spot. In Genesis 3:2-3 we read, "And the woman said to the serpent, 'We may eat of the fruit of the trees of the garden, but of the fruit of the tree which is in the midst of the garden, God said, 'You will not eat of it, **neither will you touch it**, lest you die." The Lord never said that touching the fruit will kill them, only the act of eating it will bring eternal death. This may seem like semantics, but Eve's "Fence Law" only added to her deception. When she touched the fruit and it didn't kill her, then it is easy to see how she would assume eating it wouldn't harm her either.

By the time of Christ, the Scribes and Jewish leaders had added tens of thousands of "Fence Laws" to the Torah making it impossible to follow. So, needless to say, God's message of love, patience, and mercy had faded from the hearts of His people. It was going to take some pretty radical love to win their hearts out of the hands of a well-entrenched enemy. As hard as this may be to hear (if you are hearing this for the first time), the Gospels were originally written for the Jews. The Lord's heart for His people whom He had set apart (remember the Tzitzit's) had not changed, and He wanted so much for them to see and understand the fulfillment of what He had promised them. As you read through the Gospels, you'll notice that there is multiple references to the Torah, Old Testament, as well as the Lord's feasts. These concepts would have been very foreign to the Gentiles/Greeks, who did not have the previous knowledge that the Jews were given. With that in mind, the Lord spends the entirety of the Gospels reminding them of what He had said and done to prepare them for this very moment. With all this in mind, let's look at the life and love of God through the eyes of a forgiven thief, liar, and tax collector.

The birth of Christ is one of the most widely celebrated events in the world. Yet, paganism, commercialism, and humanism have crept in and greatly distracted from not only the total miracle of His coming, but the absolute perfection of His timing and why the date is so important. Mark Biltz did a fascinating study on this topic which can be found on Youtube, but I am only going to highlight the points found in the Word rather than try to cover his entire study. In Deuteronomy 16:16 we read, "Three times in a year all of you males will appear before the Lord your God in a place which He will choose during the Feast of Unleavened Bread, in the Feast of Weeks, and in the Feast of Sukkot..." If you watch Mark Biltz' study, you will find that Christ was born on the first day of the Feast of Sukkot (or Tabernacle) based on the prophesy of John the Baptist's birth. What makes this so powerful is the scripture in Deuteronomy that we just read. The Jews were commanded by God to be "in a place which He will choose" which would later become Jerusalem.

So it wasn't necessarily the census that brought the Jewish people and left no room in the inns, but a Torah commandment of God. To make this even more remarkable, we have to look back at the commandment for the Feast of Sukkot. In Deuteronomy 16:14-15 the Lord says, "And you will rejoice in your feast, you, your son, your daughter, your manservant, your maidservant, the Levite, the stranger, the fatherless, and the widow who are within your gates. You will keep a solemn feast to the Lord your God for seven days in the place which the Lord will choose, because the Lord your God will bless you in all your increase and in all the works of your hands, therefore you will surely rejoice." The Lord had created a feast that would have all of His people in the perfect place, and at the perfect time for the birth of His Son! If you remember from earlier, we found that "Mo'ed" or feast was also defined as "divine appointment." If you are a student of history (which I am working on), you know that this was not a new time to celebrate the birth of Christ, but it was actually common practice by the Messianic Jews until the reign of the Roman Emperor Constantine.

It is not hard to wrap our minds around the fact that the Lord really doesn't need us to fulfill all that He has planned. However, it is that He greatly desires for us to play a crucial role, which demonstrates just how much He loves us! Not only that, what glory does He receive if we don't know what He has done or is doing? He even sent prophets after the writing of the Torah to tell where and how the Christ was going to be born. Isaiah 7:14 reads, "Behold a virgin will be pregnant and will bear a son, and they will call His Emanuel;" and Micah 5:1 reads, "But you, Bethlehem Ephratah, though you are small among the thousands of Judah, yet out of you One will come forth to Me Who is to be ruler in Israel, Whose goings forth are from of old, from everlasting." Matthew refers to both of these passages in the first chapter of his account; which again, only the Jews would have had knowledge of at the time. Matthew's account would have been very long if he had cited every scripture that proclaimed the coming of Christ. In his book "Wild at Heart," John Eldridge likens the birth of Christ as "an invasion into enemy occupied territory." The Groom had returned for His bride like a knight racing into the Dragon's lair to rescue his princess.

We all love the stories of the Hero risking life and limb, and overcoming seemingly impossible odds to win back his true love. Well, I am pleased to announce that we have been grafted into just such a story.

Loving against the Grain:

As I said earlier, the world Christ was born into had changed drastically from the days of Abraham, Isaac, and Jacob. Relationships and wonders had been replaced with religious regulations and traditions. Men (as we so often do) believed that they had cornered the market on the Word, and they alone had the authority to tell people how to communicate with God. I wish it were not so, but we see this trend repeated throughout history to this very day. Slowly over time, the intimacy with God had faded away and now a relationship with Him seemed to be quite the burden to bare. So it's no wonder that Y'shua's approach from the very beginning was the direct opposite of what the leaders of the time were teaching. For starters, Y'shua allowed Himself to be baptized (Mikvah) by John the Baptist (or the "immerser" in the literal translation) who the Pharisees and Sadducees at the time thought was a mad man. Here John is a high priest of Israel by birth; but instead of following in his father's footsteps and serving in the Holy of Holies, he decides to wear camel skins, live in the wilderness, and eat wild locus and honey. (For those of you that may be confused about the John's diet and the Torah requirements conflicting, "locus" was also the name of a plant eaten in that region.) Not to mention John often referred to the religious leaders of that time as the "Offspring of vipers" (Mat. 3:7), so he probably wasn't invited over for dinner very often. With that being said, for Y'shua to seek John out and have him baptize Him must have put a pretty bad taste in the mouths of the religious leaders. What the religious leaders failed to see was that John was the fulfillment of Isaiah's prophecy in Isaiah 40:3 when he wrote, "A voice crying out in the wilderness; You must right now prepare the way of the Lord, you must continually make His path straight." Where the religious leaders saw a mad man, Y'shua saw a faithful servant doing exactly what he was called to do.

    I believe that obedience is one of the greatest ways we can show our King just how much we love Him, and John had been declaring that love for all of this adult life. Y'shua didn't care about what having a relationship with John would do to His social status; He loved John and He wanted to include him into His plan. We know that Christ was not baptized for the remission of His sins, but so He could "fulfill all righteousness" (Mat. 3:15). Y'shua wanted to be in right standing with His Father in every area of His life; and just as we saw with Abraham and Isaac, He will never tell us to do something that He Himself has not done. In this same passage of scripture we read, "And after Y'shua was immersed He immediately rose from the water: and behold the heavens opened up to Him, and he saw the Spirit of God descending like a dove and coming upon Him: and there was a voice from the heavens saying, 'This is My beloved Son, with Whom I am well pleased." What an incredible sight this must have been for all who were in attendance including John. Not only did they get to hear the Lord declare Who Y'shua was, but that Y'shua was His and He loved Him. The concept of a relationship with God had just been rekindled before their very eyes. This seemingly distant and unsatisfied God was suddenly declaring that He loved someone and He was pleased with Him.

    This is probably the hardest truth for us to grasp at a heart level, that we are loved and He is pleased with us. We are His creation and He said that we are "good." When we are struggling with sin, He loves us still and loves us enough not to leave us there. Again, the whole concept of being able to have a personal relationship with God must have been absolutely mind blowing. An even deeper revelation for them was that the Lord wanted that relationship just as badly as they did. Not only would this have challenged what they were taught about the Lord, but also about what they were taught when it comes to who they are to Him. Another area where the enemy loves to attack us is our identity in Christ. I have heard it said in New Age circles that we should all be on a journey to find our "true selves." When in reality, that "true" identity can only be found in Christ and His love for us. It is His love, His mercy, and His redemptive power that has given us our value. A clear example of this was when Y'shua was lead into the wilderness in Matthew 4. In verses 3-4 we read, "And when the one who was testing, the devil came, he said, 'If you are the Son of God, You must now say that these stones would become bread. But when He answered, Y'shua said, 'It is written, Man will not live on bread alone, but upon every word going out through the mouth of God." Notice how the enemy starts his first attack against Christ, "If you are the Son of God..." This is clearly a challenge to His identity and an attempt to make Christ prove Himself. Isn't it interesting how Y'shua's identity was established by God and then immediately challenged by Satan? With that in mind, Y'shua's response should take on a whole new meaning for us. Christ declared to the enemy in quoting Deut. 8:3 that "I don't need to turn rocks into bread to convince you or Me of My identity; but I live by every word that comes from the mouth of my Father, and He has proclaimed who I am."

The very next temptation of Y'shua follows the exact same pattern as the first. In verses 5-7 we read, "Then the devil took him to the holy city and placed Him on the pinnacle of the Temple and said to Him, 'If you are the Son of God, You must throw Yourself down at once for it has been written that He will give orders to His angels concerning you and they will take you up in the palms of their hands, so that you would not strike your foot against a stone.' Y'shua said to him, 'Again it is written, You will not test the Lord your God." Again, we see the enemy use the challenging phrase "If you are the Son of God," but this time he is trying to bring into question Y'shua's identity in God's love for Him. Once again Y'shua quotes the Torah and tells the enemy that God's love doesn't have to be proven to him; He has already declared that Christ was His "beloved." The final temptation of the enemy may not seem like an attack at who Christ is, but again the pattern remains the same. In verses 8-10 we read, "Again the devil took Him to an exceedingly high mountain and showed Him all the kingdoms of the world and their glory and said to Him, 'I shall give you all these things to You, if after You will fall on Your knees You would pay homage to me.' Then Y'shua said to him, 'You must immediately go back to where you came from, Satan: for it has been written, You will worship the Lord your God and you will serve only Him." As before, Y'shua chooses a passage out of Deuteronomy (6:13) to combat the lies of the enemy. I find it interesting that Y'shua didn't use some powerful prayer that none of the people at that time would have known, but rather He chose passages that the Jews would have been very familiar with.

As far as this being yet another attack on Christ's identity; if you remember, the Lord has already proclaimed that Y'shua was His Son in Whom He was well pleased. So this is a test to see if the Y'shua believed that the Lord would truly give Him all that was promised in the writing of the prophets before this time. So the question here is "are You truly God's Son or just His servant," because servants don't receive an inheritance. Y'shua responds by reminding Satan as to Who the true worship belongs; that again, the Lord has already declared that He is His Son.

We cannot forget who we are in Christ and what He has already declared over our own lives. When we begin to question His love for us, fear, doubt, and a self-destructive spirit will follow closely afterwards.

A God of Second Chances:

Now that Y'shua has been filled with the spirit and overcome the challenge made to His identity, He is now ready to begin His earthly ministry and He starts it off with a bang! As Christ is walking down the shore of Galilee, He sees Simon Peter and Andrew his brother casting their nets into the lake. Both men were professional fishermen, they had a business to run, and they have already made a decent investment into their business seeing how they had a boat. Then suddenly in an act that seems very strange, Y'shua tells them in Matthew 4:19 "You must come after Me, and I shall make you fishers of men." Then without any hesitation the Bible says, "And immediately, having left their nets, they followed Him." For anyone who has or currently does own their own business, this would seem absolutely nuts. A man you have never met comes walking up and tells you to follow them, and you simply drop everything and do it. Some would argue that they followed

Him because He was Y'shua the Christ. Yet if you remember, the revelation as to Who Christ is wasn't shown to them until later on. This is where a cultural disconnect can leave us scratching our heads about their sudden change of careers; but the truth is, there is something pretty powerful happening here that has never happened before.

In a Contextual Reflection from Preserving Bible Time titled *"Follow Me"* by Doug Greenwold, we get a pretty incredible insight as to what is taking place and why what Christ did meant so much. During this time in the Jewish culture, Rabbis were held in a place of high honor and esteem. For lack of a better term, they were the "Rock Stars" of their times that nearly every Jewish boy strived to become. According to the "Follow Me" article, Jewish boys began their training at age five in their local synagogue schools to learn Hebrew and memorize (yes, memorize) the Torah. By the time the student was thirteen, the best and brightest students would have the Torah, The Prophets, and the Writings (which comprised of all of the Hebrew Scripture) completely contributed to memory. That simple fact alone seems so far beyond human comprehension, and it convicts me when it comes to my scriptural memorization. Per the article, the best and brightest would "study the wisdom and authoritative interpretation of the Torah by the sages known as the 'Yoke of Torah'." They would then follow Rabbis until they were twenty years of age to help "hone their ability to interpret God's Word as it relates to all the practical issues of daily life." The up-and-coming disciple would then have to choose carefully which Rabbi they want to commit to following. Some rabbis had a very literal approach to the Torah, whereas others were more interpretive. When the student finally picked which rabbi he wished to follow, he would ask the rabbi if he could be his disciple, and in a sense, take on the "yoke of the rabbi." The rabbi would then grill the disciple on scriptural knowledge and understanding, and he would only select a very elect few. The disciples would, in turn be a representation of the rabbi; per the "Follow Me" article, the rabbis wanted to make sure that the disciples could be "just like him." Once the student passed the litany of questions in the interview process, he hears the words that he has longed to hear since he was five years old: "Come, follow me."

    The next question you should be asking yourself is: "what happens to the students who fell short of this strenuous process?" The answer is that they would go home and pick up their family's trait and begin working. So what does this tell you about all of the disciples that Christ chose? They were all failed rabbis! Now, there is a very good chance that they knew Christ was a well-known and respected teacher who had no disciples at that time. He is referred to as such throughout the gospels; if you remember in Luke 2:46-49, Mary and Joseph find a 13-year-old Christ sitting and speaking with the teachers. As He asked and answered their questions, verse 47 says "and all those who heard Him were amazed over His understanding and answers." So it is reasonable to assume that Christ became a rabbi at a young age in comparison to His peers, and the word of this rare accomplishment had gotten around. So when Peter and Andrew saw Christ, I am sure that the last thought going through their minds would be to ask this Master of scripture if they could be His disciples. Yet, to their utter shock and amazement, Christ asked them to follow Him. No wonder they dropped everything and came running. They had been given a second chance at a life they just knew had passed them by. Can you imagine the value Peter, Andrew, James, and John must have felt when Y'shua called them? I am sure their minds were racing to find what incredible potential and faith that Christ saw in them that they themselves had failed to realize. When in reality all He saw was willing, empty vessels for Him to fill. He wasn't so much concerned about what they knew or what they could do, but rather He knew what He was able to do through them. I have heard it said that "God doesn't call the qualified; He qualifies the called." He sought out those that the modern church had rejected, so they could see the perfection of His love working in imperfect people. What better way to convey the kind of people He was coming to save and set apart, than to pour Himself into the least of these in the religious word. I have also heard it said that those who have been forgiven much love much. They truly understand the weight of what was done for them, and so it is easier for them to show that same mercy to others that they themselves do desperately needed.

Y'shua and His Torah:

In the 5th chapter of Matthew, we find Y'shua teach the famous sermon on the Mount which is so well known by many. Most have focused on "The Beatitudes" and rightfully so since there are many precious promises found in these passages. Yet, there is a portion of scripture that seems to be read over rather quickly, and I believe it is because there is not a lot of understanding in its meaning. In Matthew 5:17-19 we read, "Do not think that I came to do away with, or to bring an incorrect interpretation to, the Torah or the Prophets: I did not come to do away with but to bring spiritual abundance, for the Torah (Teachings) to be obeyed as it should be and God's promises to receive fulfillment. For truly I say to you: until the sky and the Earth would pass away, not one yod or one vav could ever pass away from the Torah (Teaching), until everything would come to pass." I believe where the confusion comes in can be found in other translations that read that the Law has been fulfilled. I do not believe that the Lord was doing away with half of the Word because He is the Word. The "spiritual abundance" is found in the understanding that everything that the Lord had Israel doing in the Old Testament was soon to be revealed in Him.

As I have mentioned before, it was the generational obedience of Israel (even though they fell short many times) that would later proclaim Christ to His people. The Lord had commanded to Israel what He wanted them to do, and He was revealing through Y'shua why He had them do it. This is where the deception comes in when it comes to the value of Torah. The enemy would have us believe that it is simply a bunch of old laws that Christ got rid of, and that they should not be a part of our studies or walk.

As we have seen with the Feast alone, nothing could be further from the truth and Y'shua is reaffirming that here. All of the Word is to be given equal value in order to have an accurate picture of God's love for us. By discarding Torah (and in some cases the Old Testament as a whole) we greatly hinder the foundation of our knowledge of Him and what He did for us. In a sense, we know what Y'shua did for us, but we just don't fully understand why. As we go through the Gospels, you will see how Y'shua continues to bring the Jewish people's minds back to the scriptures that they had studied for so long. Except this time, they are seeing why following these commands meant so much to Him at the time. If not for the Feast of Tabernacle, the Feast of Unleavened Bread, and the Feast of Pentecost, a good portion of the Jewish people would not have been in Israel to see Christ's death, burial, resurrection, or the out pouring of the Holy Spirt. The Torah and the prophets were instrumental in preparing the way for Y'shua's ministry thousands of years before His miraculous birth, and He did not want them to miss these truths and revelations. Be not deceived; the Lord has a plan and a purpose for every eternal word He put in His scriptures and they cannot be discarded. What Christ was teaching was twisted into appearing that He was teaching against the "Law of Moses;" but in truth, He was slowly replacing their understanding of what was written with why it was written. This is known as teaching the spirit of the law and not just the letter of it, or bringing "spiritual abundance."

When I was a kid, I used to drive my parents nuts by asking a simple question over and over again: why? They would tell me to do something and if I didn't see the purpose in it, I would ask for the reasoning behind the request instead of just doing what I was asked. More often than not, I would get the ever famous response of "Because I said so!" Needless to say, this would not answer my question (not that there was one that would make me want to clean my room), but I would then do it out of obligation and would commit half of my efforts to the task. As Christ was teaching on the mount, this was more than likely the mindset of the people He was speaking to. A people who had been under Sadducee and Pharisee law that was driven purely by "Devine Obligation" rather than love. So when Christ proclaimed that He had come to bring fulfillment, maximum understanding, or spiritual abundance (whichever translation your Bible has) this is what He meant and what an eye opening revelation that must have been for them. No longer was it a "Because I said so," but instead; a "do this so you will know Me and My love for you" mindset. It is similar to having a conversation with your kids about drugs, drinking, or fornication; if you come at it from the angle of demanded obedience, chances are you are going to drive them straight to the things you want them to avoid. Yet, if you present it from the prospective of love and protection, you will have a much greater chance for success. When your child is presented with the temptation, they won't think "I can't because mom, dad, and God will be mad at me," but "I can't because those who adore me said that it would cause me physical and spiritual harm, and I don't want to hurt them or me." Can you see how incredibly powerful that simple change in approach can be? Y'shua was trying to convey to Israel the same change in mindset. I can almost hear Him saying, "Don't do it to appease God; do it because you love Me, because I love you, and by doing these things you will be ever reminded of that love."

Now I must add a word of caution as you begin to study the scriptures with this new approach: the enemy hates it with a passion. He will quickly attempt to get you to fall into the slippery pit of self-righteousness and salvation through works. The enemy loves getting people lost in the letter of the God's commands, while causing them to lose the spirit behind the command. Never lose track of the "why," because He loves us and He wants us to be reminded of that love constantly.

Matters of the Heart:

     I have heard it said that there is more grace in the "New Testament" than there was in the old, and in some respects I can see how many would come to that conclusion. However, when it came to the meditations of the heart, Y'shua takes a much stricter stance in the New Testament. In Matthew 5:21-22 we read, "You have heard it said to the ancients, 'Do not murder:' and whoever would murder, that one would be guilty in the judgement. And I say to you that everyone who is angry with his brother will be guilty of judgement." We see this same addressing of the heart in Matthew 5:27-28, "You have heard it said, 'You will not commit adultery.' But I am saying to you that everyone who looks at a woman with desire for her has already committed adultery with her in his heart." Y'shua is, of course, referring back to the Ten Commandments (or statements) found in Exodus 20, which all of the people would have been very familiar with.

     Yet Christ knew that, with the relationship He was wanting to establish with them, physical obedience was no longer going to be enough. Their hearts had to be right in order for them to replicate the kind of love Y'shua was demonstrating. Between these two issues of the heart, the one that can be the most crippling (especially for guys) is the one of purity. We are so deceived into thinking that as long as we do not act on our thoughts, then we are not doing anything wrong. I have had guy friends in the past say, "It is ok if you look at the menu, as long as you don't buy anything." Absolutely nothing could be further from the truth. Just ask King David when he saw Bathsheba, or King Solomon when he was led astray by his many pagan wives and mistresses. In this area of struggle, again the enemy tries to get us to stay surface deep as to its importance and its effect on our lives as a whole. He tries to make us think, "ok, ok, I know it is sin. But everyone sins and it is not that big of a deal. It's just what guys do." The significance of purity reaches so much farther than most of us have been taught or are willing to receive. To fully grasp why this sin of the heart means so much to the Lord, we first have to understand what the Lord is trying to accomplish in us, and it is not simply to "be a better Christian." He is trying to create in us a maturity that not only helps us to overcome temptation, but instill in us strength that is greater than the desires of our flesh.

Again, this is where having a knowledge of Torah helps to convey the message that the Lord is trying to drive home. If you remember when we were in Exodus 35:30-40:38, the Lord commanded Moses and the children of Israel to build the Tabernacle, and He went into great detail on how He wanted it built. If you also remember we then saw how by building the Tabernacle, they were creating a visual representation of Christ. To top it all off, in Exodus 40 we read how the glory of the Lord came down and filled the temple as a cloud by day and fire by night. So how does the Tabernacle in Exodus apply to sexual sin in the New Testament? We find the answer in Romans 8:11, "And if the Spirit of the One Who raised Y'shua from the dead dwells in you, the One Who raised Messiah from the dead will also make alive your mortal bodies through His Spirit because He abides within you." In Exodus, the Tabernacle was a representation of Christ and a place where men could enter into the presence of God and not be consumed. Here in Matthew, Y'shua is trying to prepare their (and our) hearts because they were now the Tabernacles! In the scripture we just read in Romans, the word "abides" means to live or dwell in. If our bodies are the Tabernacles where sacrifices are made, where worship and the incense of our praise is offered, then our hearts are the Holy of Holies! It is where our own Arks of the Covenant was kept, filled with reminders of God's faithfulness to us in the most personal of ways. It is for this reason that Y'shua had to make sure His children understood the importance of the conditions of their hearts. He was trying to prepare them for the time when He no longer tabernacles with them, but within them. Just as it is written in Exodus 40, the Lord wants to fill the Temples of our flesh and the sacred places of our hearts with His glory. Sexual sin and the lust of the heart is a direct attack on this entire process, and it is designed to hinder it from coming to pass on every front. To make matters worse, this sin convinces us that we are not worth or deserving of such a filling.

We begin to believe that we are not worthy of His love or that the Lord would want nothing to do with a Temple so filthy. In reality, He was standing next to you while you were in the midst of committing the sin you are so ashamed of. The truth is He loves you just as He did before you fell. The Lord knows better than we ever could, that the meditations of the heart are what gives birth to sin. That is why He is telling all of us to cut the sin off at its source, and to not allow it the opportunity to manifest in our lives. We are the Tabernacle He is longing to fill; it is the sacrifices of our hearts and our praise that He desires to consume with fire. And He is the One Who wants to walk us through the cleansing and restorative process so He can dwell fully in our hearts and minds.

Washed Clean:

I know I have said this many times already, but it is a point that I find so powerful and so comforting at the same time. God will always do it (whatever the need) in a way that we will know it was Him. Here is yet another miracle where the Lord used Torah to declare who Y'shua was. As Christ finishes His sermon on the mount, a huge crowd follows Him as He is walking down and is approached by a leper. We read in Matthew 8:2-4, "And behold, when a leper came he was kneeling before Him saying, 'Lord, if you would be willing, You are able to cleanse me.' Then as He stretched out His hand He touched him saying, 'I am willing, you must instantly be cleansed.' And his leprosy was immediately cleansed. Then Y'shua said to him, 'You must see that you would not tell anyone, but you must go, show yourself to the priest and present the offering which Moses commanded, in testimony to them.'" From a Hebrew perspective, there is so much that took place in this brief encounter that its mind-blowing. First, let's look at what appears to be Christ violating Torah in front of a large crowd of Torah followers. Both chapter 13 and 14 of Leviticus go into extensive detail as to how a priest can determine if a person has leprosy, the proper steps for determining when they are not contagious, and how to quarantine them while they are. The Lord even goes so far as to describe how to cleanse a lepers clothing and even their house. In Numbers 5:1-3, the Lord tells the children of Israel to put people with this condition and those who have had contact with them or the dead out of the camp.

It is easy to see that touching someone with this condition would violates God's order of clean and unclean. In fact, the process to be proclaimed clean again is eight day's longs and requires shaving off all of your body hair, and offering both animal and oil sacrifices. So why is it that Christ told the man He healed to go and perform this cleansing process, but He Himself did not have to? The answer is what you would expect from a God that is absolutely and completely in control, and has been from the very beginning. Exodus 29:37 says, "Seven days you shall make an atonement for the alter, and sanctify it; and it shall be an altar most holy; whatever touches the altar shall be holy." Then again in Leviticus 6:20, we see that whatever touches the flesh of the sin offering becomes holy! Christ did not have to be cleansed because He was (and is) our sin offering! For thousands of years, animals have been the sacrifice for sin. Now, these first century Jews are having to wrap their minds around the fact that a man could be their sin offering.

You'll also notice that Christ told the leper to go present himself to the priest so it would be a "testimony to them." It only stands to reason that if the Lord gave commandments on how to proclaim a leper clean again, then people have recovered from this disease before. So why would this be any different from any other leper who has been proclaimed clean? I believe that the answer lies within the actual condition itself and the mindset of the people at this time. For the first century Jewish people, it was often believed that there was a direct link between leprosy and sin. If we look at a couple of examples in the Old Testament, it is easy to see why this would be so commonly believed. In Exodus 12, the Lord's anger was kindled against Aaron and Miriam for speaking against Moses. In verse 9-10 we read, "And the anger of the Lord was kindled against them and He departed. And the cloud left from the Tabernacle and, behold, Miriam became leprous, white as snow and Aaron looked at Miriam and, behold, she was leprous." Then there is the account of Naaman in 2 Kings 5, where Elisha tells Naaman in verse

10 to "...immerse in the Jordan seven times and your flesh will come again to you and you will be clean." The key thing to note in this passage about Naaman is the immersing seven times to cleanse his leprosy, this is called a "Mikveh" in Hebrew and it is done for purification. Finally, another interesting scripture to support this mindset can be found in Leviticus 13:12-13. It reads, "And if leprosy breaks out abroad in the skin and the leprosy covers all his skin that has the plague from his head even to his foot, wherever the priest looks, then the priest will consider and, behold, if the leprosy has covered all his flesh, he will pronounce him clean that has the plague: it is all turned white, he is clean."

    So here lies again what looks like a contradiction of scripture. In the earlier verses of Chapter 13, the Bible says that if a person has a bright spot, then he is unclean; if he is covered head to toe, he is clean. I believe that the answer to this dilemma can be found in an article by R.G. Cochrane M.D., and brings an incredible revelation into the story of the leper who Christ healed. Dr. Cochrane was a Consultant Leprologist, a Technical Medical Adviser; he worked with the American Leprosy Missions Inc., and was formerly the Principle of the Christian Medical College in Vellore, Madras, and India. In his 1961 article *"Biblical Leprosy: A Suggested Interpretation,"* Dr. Cochrane makes the argument that what we have read as leprosy in the Bible all these years may not have been leprosy at all. According to Dr. Cochrane, the earliest and most accurate account of clinical leprosy did not appear until 600 BC in

China. He believed that this term was given to a broad variety of skin conditions from rashes to psoriasis, but none of the conditions correctly described leprosy. Dr. Cochrane said that what made this lack of correct description so interesting was the fact that early Babylonian writing described conditions like epilepsy very well. Finally, Dr. Cochrane said that through his research, he found that the most common Hebrew word translated as leprosy is "Tsara'ath," which is more accurately translated as "defiled or stricken." Both translations would suggest that this condition was brought upon someone through a curse associated with disobedience. I believe that through Dr. Cochrane's research, it is reasonable to believe that these diseases were like a physical manifestation of sin! Moreover, nothing is more contagious than sin. Christ didn't just want the leper to go through the purification process to obey Torah; He wanted the leper to declare to the priest that his sin had been washed away! What a thought that Y'shua wanted to bless not only the leper, but the priest of the time as well.

    Despite all of the scientific explanation as to what the Y'shua did in this miracle, there is something very personal about it as well. Christ could have just as easily spoke to the cursed man's body and made it clean, so why didn't He? Why stir up those around Him with what appeared to be a clear violation of Torah when it came to unclean things? The answer? Because it is what would mean the most to the leper's heart. What engaging love that the Lord would establish commandments for dealing with sin, and then Christ would come in the form of the answer for all of it. He was the only one who could touch the untouchable, reach the unreachable, and all of it was by design. The Lord came in a form that would not only take away our sin, but a form that would allow Him to have close and meaningful contact with us while remaining Holy. How many times do we feel so unclean that we dare not approach a pure and undefiled God? Yet, His plan all along was to create provisions for His love for us no matter what we do. When He holds the dirty, they can sense His love and they desire to be clean. He does not condemn them into obligated obedience; instead, He shows what unconditional love looks like. It is not enough for the Lord to simply help us in our time of need; He wants His acts to mean something to us on a heart level so that the affect will be eternal.

Love over sacrifice:

As we continue through Christ's legacy of love in Matthew chapter 9, we find the Lord calling Matthew to be one of His disciples. Again, if you were to stop and look at the people Y'shua was choosing to represent him, Matthew was a PR nightmare. Matthew was a Jewish man who worked for the Romans to collect taxes from his own people. So to say that he was hated would probably be a gross understatement. Yet, if you remember the process it took to become a disciple, Matthew would have been another example of someone who did not come close to meeting the requirements. I have to remind myself that the Lord doesn't call the qualified; He qualifies the called. This is done so that the called will be blessed and radically changed, and so that the Lord will receive all of the glory. I also try to keep this principle in mind so I do not begin to trust or glory in my own knowledge. The Lord didn't call me because of my incredible ability, but because all would know that there is no way I could have done it without Him.

Right after Matthew tells of his own calling, he notes a powerful exchange between Y'shua and the Pharisees. In Matthew 9:10-13 we read, "And it happened while He was reclining in his house, then there were many tax collectors and sinners who came and they were reclining at the table with Y'shua and His disciples. And when the Pharisees saw them they were saying to His disciples, 'Why does your Teacher eat with the tax collectors and sinners?' Then since He heard He said, 'The strong have no need of a physician, but those who are evil (or the sick in Latin). But when you go what you must learn is, I desire loving Kindness and not sacrifice: for I did not come to call the righteous but the sinners." Can you see the wide spread affect the calling of Matthew is already having on those around him? The Bible said that there were many tax collectors and sinners who came to sit with Christ. They knew that if Christ could save and change Matthew, then they had a chance for a new life as well.

Again, it was the living testimony of Matthew and not the ability that Y'shua was after. You will also notice that Christ didn't just "hang out" with sinners. He dwelled with those who were truly repentant and were seeking a new life. An example of this can be seen in who He rebuked and who He ministered too. The Pharisees and Sadducees normally caught the brunt of Christ's righteous anger while the broken, the hurting, and those who were truly seeking saw His love and mercy. All of them were "sinners," but the Lord knew the differences concerning their hearts and their intents. The response that Y'shua gave those who were murmuring against Him must have blown their minds. When He said in verse 13 that He "desired loving kindness and not sacrifice...," two very powerful truths were declared. First, He was reaffirming Who He was and we know this because why would you offer sacrifices to a man, or what kind of man would suggest that sacrifices have been made to him? Secondly, that He had not come to call the righteous but the sinners. This must have been a complete 180 from everything the religious leaders of the time were trained to believe. They were supposed to be the "Elite," the ones that God loved and favored most. Yet, here is Christ telling them that He was more concerned about the tax collectors and sinners that were with Him.

    As we have seen before many times, the word that jumps out of this passage is "loving kindness" or "Hesed." The Lord is not concerned about their offerings; He wants to see acts of love that goes far beyond what is required of it. To reaffirm that this has been the Lord's heart throughout scripture and not just a "New Testament concept," look at what is written in Hosea 6:6. It reads, "For I desire loving kindness and not sacrifice, and the knowledge of God more than burnt offerings." The Lord does not care about how "holy" we appear or what tremendous sacrifices we make; if it is not done out of love and compassion towards others, then it is worthless and profits us nothing. The prophet Isaiah said it best in Isaiah 64:5-6, "But we are all as an unclean thing, and all our acts of loving kindness are like a filthy garment. And we all fade like a leaf, and our iniquities, like the wind, have taken us away. And there is no one who calls upon Your name, who stirs himself up to take hold of You, for You have hidden Your face from us, and have consumed us, because of our iniquities."

The power of a Word:

There is nothing like receiving a word or a promise from the Lord that is unique to our situation. We could be in the pit of despair, overwhelmed by circumstances, and then He whispers a word into our spirit and suddenly we can face anything. As we continue in Matthew, we see an example of the power of clinging to a promise. What makes this another revelation of God's heart is the fact that, in order to be healed, the believer had to physically touch Him. The account can be found in Matthew 9:20

which reads, "And there was a woman, who was suffering with a Hemorrhage for twelve years, when she came up behind Him she touched the fringe of His prayer shawl: for she was saying within herself 'If only I could touch his prayer shawl I will be delivered.' And when Y'shua turned around and saw her He said, 'Be of good cheer daughter: for your faith has delivered you.' And the woman was delivered from that moment." I have heard this account, as I am sure you have many times before, and it has been taught from the perspective of persevering faith. Though this is an accurate teaching, there is so much more to it than what is on the surface. First, many translations have worded this passage as the woman grabbed the "hem" of His garment, which is a loose translation since they did not hem their garments during this time. Second, you will notice that in the translation I am using (the One New Man Bible) that it says that she "touched the fringe of His prayer shawl." This may seem like semantics, but the wording here is crucial because it ties this event with three other passages, which gives the full picture of what took place.

The first passage we have discussed before in Numbers 15:37-41 which reads, "And the Lord spoke to Moses saying, 'Speak to the children of Israel and bid them to make fringes for themselves in the wings of their garments throughout their generations and that they put upon the fringe of the border a thread of blue, and it will be to you for a fringe, that you may look upon it and remember all the commandments of the Lord and do them, and that you do not seek after your own heart and your own eyes, after which you use to go astray, so you will remember and do all My commandments and be holy to your God. I AM the LORD you God, Who brought you out of the land of Egypt, to be your God: I AM the LORD your God." So this fringe had very significant meaning to the Jewish people; and of course, Christ would have been wearing them to stay in compliance with His own commandment. The next passage can be found in Malachi 3:20, "But to you who revere My name, the Sun of Acts of Loving Kindness will rise with healing in His wings and you will go out and prosper like fattening calves in the stall." This passage may not be so obvious as to how it applies to the woman with the issue of blood, but this is the very promise she was clinging to.

    According to William Morford, the Hebrew verb used for "The Sun of Acts of Loving Kindness rising" is "Zerah" which likens the rising of the sun to the glory of God. Next is the part of the passage which talks about "healing in His Wings," and the explanation of this can be found in Deuteronomy 22:12. "You will make for yourself fringes upon the four corners of your prayer shawl with which you cover yourself." The word for corners, border, or quarters (whichever translation you have) in the Hebrew is "kanaph" and translates in Strong's H3671 as A WING! So the fringe (or tsitsit) which she grabbed was attached to the "wings" of His prayer shawl. I believe that the woman with the issue of blood knew, understood, and believed the scriptures and it was what drove her to grab the fringe on the wing of Y'shua's garment. This belief is reaffirmed later on in Matthew 14:34-36, which says "Then after they crossed they came to shore in Gennesaret. And when they recognized Him the men of that place sent into that whole neighboring region and they brought to Him all those who had evil and they were begging Him to just touch the tsitsit of His prayer shawl: and they who touched were rescued."

What a beautiful way to heal. It is almost as if the Lord is saying, "I don't just want you to seek, or declare My Word; I want you touch me and know that I am good." This is the power that is found in clinging to a word from God. Not only did the woman with an issue of blood find her healing, but her actions declared to the surrounding regions that we serve a God we can touch. Moreover, we serve a God who desires that level of contact and relationship with us. For years, the Jewish people were taught the difference between clean and unclean, and how the two were not to have any contact. Now, they are witnessing with their own eyes the clean desiring the unclean. Again, how wonderful is our God that He would come in a form that could be touched by all and still remain holy, and that this was His plan all along.

A hands on approach:

What better way for Y'shua to demonstrate his love than to empower others to do the same. As we continue in Matthew's writings in chapter 10, we see Christ sending His twelve disciples out to preach to the "lost sheep of Israel" and do everything He did. If Christ's heart was purely after His own fame and glory, He would have kept His ministry a one man show. Instead, He replicates Himself in His disciples and sends them out two by two to broaden His ministry of love and service. Not only did the Lord want to show them His ability to work through them, but there is a new depth of love and satisfaction that comes from heart felt acts of service. He wanted His disciples to know what it was like to instill hope where there was none; to not just see answered prayers, but to be the answer to the prayers of others. It was this kind of love that made Christ's ministry explode the way it did. It wasn't because of a bunch of wonders and magic tricks; it was the heart behind the actions. It was the ultimate word of mouth network-marketing business, whose product was physical/spiritual healing and unconditional love. What was the profit that was gain? The souls of millions that would spend an eternity with a God that adored them.

So the questions I often find myself asking is: why is it so hard for me or others to ask for help? If this was the

Lord's heart from the beginning, then why do I allow the enemy to convince me that I would just be a burden to others? We know the way we feel when we are able to step in and fill the gap for someone who needs it most, so why do we think that the feeling will not be the same for those who are helping us? The Lord never created us to be islands in this life. We were created to establish relationships, by a God who created the concept of relationships. In fact, the sole purpose for us being created was so that the Lord could have a relationship with us. Christ did not perform His ministry alone, although He easily could have. He wanted the fellowship and to demonstrate what it meant to make true, heart level connections with others. This was also demonstrated in how Christ sent the disciples out in pairs, and what He asked of them was no small task. In Matthew 10:8 we read, "You must continually heal sickness, raise the dead, cleans lepers, cast out demons: you took freely, you must also give freely."

Now this sounds all well and good, and my mind is almost tempted to picture the big healing conferences you see on TV when I read this passage. Yet, as you continue reading in chapter 10, you begin to see a different level of fellowship that is not often taught. Christ tells them about the persecutions they will have to endure during this time. He tells them how they will be drug before religious and political leaders, beaten, and may even be put to death for their faith. This brings us to a type of relationship that can only be described as a fellowship of suffering.

Though I, myself, have never had the privilege to serve in the military, I have many friends who have and I am absolutely fascinated by them. I am big into the war movies (especially the true stories) as well as war history, and it is not because I have some twisted infatuation. I know and often struggle to wrap my brain around the incredible damage and loss of life that comes from war. Yet at the same time, I am mesmerized by the stories of survival and self-sacrifice. It is the love, trust, and bond between the ones who serve together that keeps me coming back for more. There is just something about going through Hell with someone that takes a relationship to such a deeper level then just friends you hang out with every once in a while. When we look at it through that perspective, we quickly realize that we have many acquaintances, but very few friends.

I know this example will pale in comparison, but for the past six months, I have been training with a workout group called "F3." (F3nation.com) It stands for "Fitness, Fellowship, and Faith," and it is a free men's outdoor workout that has running groups, boot camps, and ruck groups that meets at 0515. Needless to say, when I first started doing this, my body was telling me it was one of the stupidest decisions I had ever made. As time went on, I noticed that my relationship with those around me was growing deeper because we were all "suffering" together. When one is struggling (normally me) someone was there to build them up and push them farther than they ever thought they could.

Since He is the creator of all levels of relationship, the Lord knew this when He sent the disciples out in pairs. They had established a relationship with Christ, but if His ministry and His message was going to be successful, He knew that they would need to learn this kind of bond and fellowship with each other. We see this principle throughout the Word in both Old and New Testament believers. From Moses and Joshua, Elijah and Elisha, to Paul and Silas, we see this example of one picking up the other and hardships only making their commitments to each other stronger.

So why do you think Christ told His followers (and us) later on in Matthew 16:24 "...If someone wants to come after Me he must deny himself and he must immediately take his cross and he must continually follow Me." He wants us to have that same level of commitment and relationship with Him that He already has towards us, a relationship that can only be developed through fire, persecution, and spiritual combat. When victories are obtained, a new level of trust and intimacy is developed that could not have been by any other means, and it should be of no surprise how the world cannot understand this concept. Take marriages for example: when trials and hardships begin to arise, the "friends of Job" will start having you question the commitment in the first place and whether or not the two are still a "good fit." When in truth, they should be encouraging the couple to endure, and that the bond that comes through victory together is worth its weight in gold. The Lord told us that in this life, we would face trials and tribulations; and to my shame, I admit that I have questioned Christ's love for me during these times. Yet, it is through these times that our greatest growth and knowledge of who He is can be found. We do not suffer because God gets bored and wants to see how much we can take, nor does He find some kind of sadistic pleasure in it. We have an enemy that is constantly testing our faith and our trust in Christ; the Lord promises that if we cling to Him and endure the attack, that which was designed to kill us will be redeemed for our good. Our walk with Him gets closer, our understanding of His ways gets sharper, our love for Him gets deeper, and our foundation in Him is even more solidified. Though we can taste of this during the "good times," it is in the fight that we truly find Him. Y'shua was establishing this concept in His disciples so when He left, their suffering would do nothing but strengthen their resolve to advance His kingdom.

      Furthermore, He wanted them to have the same level of faith, commitment, and trust in each other so the division tactics of the enemy wouldn't stand a chance. It is often taught that if you are going through a tough time in your walk, it is because you are doing something wrong or have a "secret sin." When the truth is more often than not that you are facing whatever trial because you are doing something right, and you have your cross on your shoulder right where it belongs. Moreover, you will know who your real friends are, because they will be walking next to you with their own cross, encouraging you to go just a little further.

Chapter 9

The warnings of a Friend

     As we draw ever closer to the death and resurrection of Christ, we see an aspect of His heart being repeated that I believe is often overlooked. If you remember in Genesis 18:16-18, the Lord tells Abraham what He is planning on doing to Sodom and Gomorrah which He didn't have to do. The passage reads, "And the men rose up from there and looked toward Sodom and Abraham went with them to bring them on the way. And the Lord said, 'Will I hide from Abraham that thing which I am about to do, seeing that Abraham will surely become a great and mighty nation and all the nations of the earth will be blessed in him?" This was such a powerful example of God's love towards Abraham that He would include him in what was about to happen. The Lord knew that these cities were dear to Abraham's heart and that those he loved lived there. Therefore, the Lord was preparing Abraham's heart so that His actions would not hurt their relationship. To think that a God with absolute power and authority, who doesn't need to ask for permission to do anything, would take His creation into consideration before acting is almost beyond comprehension. Yet that is exactly what Y'shua is doing here when He shows this same act of love towards His disciples, and He did it for the exact same reasons He did it for Abraham.

The Jonah sign:

If there is one account in the Bible that most believers and non-believers alike are familiar with, it would have to be the one of Jonah and the whale. It tells the journey of a rebellious prophet who would not give a warning to the Nineveh, despite being specifically told to by God. The parallels between Jonah's story and Christ is uncanny, and it makes perfect sense why the Lord would use this reference in Matthew 16:4. Here, the Pharisees and Sadducees are demanding a sign from heaven to convince them of who He was. On a side note, do you remember the temptation of Christ in the wilderness to prove His identity? Here we see that same spirit hard at work again in the religious leaders; the enemy has no new strategies towards you. Just saying. Back to the passage in Matthew that reads, "An evil and adulterous generation demands a sign, but a sign will not be given to it except the sign of Jonah. Then departing from them He went away." Just as with Abraham and Isaac, the Lord would never ask us to do something He Himself would not do. Jonah was called to proclaim a warning to Nineveh so they would have the opportunity to turn from their sin and be saved. Nineveh was an enemy of Israel, their wickedness was very well known, and they were the last people Johan believed deserved mercy. Y'shua was sent to the house of Israel who had made themselves an enemy of God, and had killed the prophets He had sent to bring them back to Him.

In both cases, the means by which their salvation would be offered was something that neither Israel or Nineveh expected. When Jonah ran from God's command, the Lord causes a great storm to come upon the sea that threatened the men who Jonah was with. With the strong Greek influence (Hellenist Jews), Roman influence, and the religious leaders twisting the Word of God for their own benefit, I believe that there was a storm raging against the relationship the Lord had desired for His people. In both accounts, the ones sent to bring the message of salvation knew that only their sacrifice would calm the storm around them. Both men knew that it was the only way to prevent lives from being lost. Jonah willingly allowed himself to be thrown into the sea, just as Christ willingly allowed Himself to be crucified at the hands of His own creation. Jonah was consumed by a large fish just as Christ was consumed by the tomb, and both were presumed to have been lost forever. Instead of being digested by the large fish, the instrument of his destruction took Jonah to the place where salvation was so desperately needed. The Pharisees and Sadducees just knew that Christ was rotting in the tomb; and yet, it took Him to the place where He could lead captivity captive and become our door to eternal life.

Finally, when both men arrived at the place they had been commanded to go, there was no denying where they had been and Who had sent them. Their very appearance rocked all who saw them; their message of love, mercy, and forgiveness spread like wildfire. Hearts were turned and the Judgement of God was satisfied. Probably one of the greatest deceptions of the enemy is that the Lord is waiting with bated breath, ready to absolutely drop the hammer on us as soon as He gets the chance. In reality, we have given more than enough reasons as to why we deserve His judgment. Instead, He bends over backwards to give us the opportunity to repent and come back to Him with open arms. Just as the people of Nineveh did not deserve a second chance, neither did the religious leaders who Y'shua was trying to warn by comparing His life to Jonah. Still, this revelation was something that the Pharisees and Sadducees would have to seek out on their own. Christ used this teaching method a lot where He would give His listeners all the information they needed, but he would allow them to find the answers. If He would have simply told them, they would have missed out on the "ah ha" moment that would remain in their memory forever.

If most of us knew that evil was about to befall one of our enemies, or simply someone who had offended us, chances are we would not go out of our way to give them a heads up. With that in mind, what a telling picture of Christ's heart that He would make this attempt with those who absolutely hated Him. It is purely out of love that this warning was given to the enemies of God; as we will see later on, it would not be the last time He tries.

A promise kept:

       I can't begin to imagine what it must have been like for the disciples to hear that Christ was going to die. There must have been a tremendous amount of fear, confusion, and disbelief after everything they had seen Him do during His ministry. They have seen the dead raised, blind eyes open, the sick healed, Peter gets the revelation of Who Christ is, and three of the disciples get to see Christ in all of His glory. Another side note to declare Christ's heart with regards to the Mount of Transfiguration: do you remember when Moses was denied entry into the promise land when he disobeyed God in front of the people? The account is found in Deuteronomy 32:48-52 where Moses is allowed to see the land, but he would not be able to enter it. Fast forward to Matthew 17:1-8 and we see the account of Christ taking Peter, James, and John up the mountain to reveal Himself to them. In verses 2-3 we read, "And He was transformed before them, and His face shone like the sun, and His garments became white as the light. And behold Moses and Elijah were seen by them conversing with Him." Out of all of the Saints that Y'shua could have called to be with Him, He chose Moses. The Lord promised Moses and the children of Israel that He would lead them to a land flowing with milk and honey. And where was Christ standing when He called Moses to join Him? In the Promise Land! Even though Moses' disobedience kept Him from entering in with the children Israel, I believe the desire of God's heart for Moses to experience the land never changed. The Lord kept His promise to Moses even in death! Moses' disobedience was no small thing either. If you remember, the Lord was trying to demonstrate the kind of relationship He wanted to have with His people. Instead, Moses crucified Christ again by striking the rock a second time rather than just speaking to it. The Lord wanted to show His people that all they would have to do is ask, and the water of His Spirit would come forth in abundance.

As I have said before, the disciples would have known the Torah teaching about Moses and would have read/heard the account of him not entering in many times before. Now they get to witness the faithfulness of God to His word in a breathtaking display of power. Y'shua was declaring that He is a promise keeping God worthy of their absolute trust, and that His mercy and loving-kindness endures forever. This event also causes me to remember the account of Abraham and Isaac in Hebrews 11:17-18; which reads, "By trusting, Abraham, when he was tested, brought Isaac and he was offering his only son, he who had received the promise, to whom it was spoken that 'Your seed will be called by Isaac, inherited by him, so he considered then that God was able to raise Isaac from the dead, from which then, figuratively speaking, he took him." Abraham believed in this level of faithfulness back in Genesis, and here is the Lord demonstrating it in Matthew. This principal that the Lord went out of His way to demonstrate and then reaffirm should encourage our spirits greatly. He is faithful to His Word and there is not a shadow of change in Him. Whatever He has spoken to you, He is faithful to complete it in His perfect timing. Y'shua selected Moses from amongst the captive, since Christ had not died yet for Moses to enter into Heaven, at a perfect time to both fulfill a promise and bring about a revelation. The Lord never does anything haphazardly; the level of purpose and revelation associated with His actions are so often far above what we could ever conceive.

    So many times in my own life, I have become frustrated and hurt because I thought that a promise had "died" due to circumstances or the passage of time. Yet as I continue to walk with Lord, I find that He continues to resurrect "Isaacs" that I had laid on the alter years before. For example, there was a time when I was ministering and leading worship quite often. Over time, doors began closing and I came to the point to where I wasn't doing much of either. I started questioning whether or not those doors would ever open again, and it started feeling like these gifts were more torments than blessings. Why give me talents and abilities, and then never give me the opportunities to flow in them? The enemy quickly started placing an image in my head of the Lord dangling a carrot in front of my face, continually jerking the desires of my heart just out of my reach. I have heard that when race horses are placed into the starting gate, their heart rate and adrenaline begin to rise as they anticipate the race that is set before them. However, if there is a false start and the gates do not open, the horses have to be let out of the back and allowed to walk to calm down. If this is not done, the horses will actually begin injuring themselves trying to jump over the starting gate. I have lost count of how many times I have injured myself spiritually, and sometimes physically, trying to get a literal "jump start" on what the Lord would have for me. Then after I was hurt, I would turn and accuse God of not knowing what He was doing or what was best for me. I would, of course, be convicted by all of the times He has shown Himself faithful in the past, and repent for both my ignorance and my arrogance. II Peter 3:9 says, "The Lord does not tarry with His promises, as some consider slowness, but He is patient with you, not wanting any to be destroyed but all to come to repentance."

He is a God who is not capable of lying, nor can He go back on His Word because He Is the Word. As I said, the Lord is declaring to Peter, James, and John that He is faithful to His promises; I believe there is an underlining truth that He was preparing their hearts to remember. The Lord was showing them that not even death can hinder His plans, a truth that their faith would be clinging to very soon.

Whom He loves, He disciplines:

      I cannot say that the thought of being disciplined by God brings much comfort. However, being left to my own devices and best guesses towards the Word is even more frightening. When we read about times when the Lord had to harshly correct His people (or us), it can be difficult to find how love plays into it. In Matthew 23, we find Y'shua tearing into the Scribes and Pharisees about the hypocrisies of their doctrine, and the unbearable burden they have placed on the Children of Israel. The Lord doesn't pull any punches either; for example in verse 13-14 we read, "And woe to you, hypocrites scribes and Pharisees, because you are closing the Kingdom of the Heavens in the sight of the people: for you are not entering and you do not permit those who would enter to come in. And woe to you, hypocrite scribes and Pharisees, because you are devouring the houses of widows and you prophesy praying long, because of this you will take greater judgement." Not quite the "come as you are, we love everyone" kind of approach to evangelism is it? The real question we should be asking ourselves is "when did rebuke stop being an act of love?"

      There is such a fear that has gripped the modern day church, and it has crippled it from being as effective as the Lord intended it to be. It is the fear of "hurting feelings" and of people not liking us. I know this seems simplistic, but when is the last time you heard a pastor passionately speak out against abortion, pornography addictions among pastors, the devastating spirit of homosexuality, or how the doctrine of "tolerance" is so greatly watering down our sensitivity to sin and conviction? We have tried so desperately to appease an enemy (Satan) who wants to kill us and his demons attack without mercy. So why do we continue to show them any whatsoever? In this incredible display of calling out leaders for what they were, you never hear Christ try to soften the blows in any way, shape, or form. He doesn't say, "I'm really sorry if this offends you, but I think what you are teaching these people is incorrect and I think we need to sit down at Starbucks and talk about it." No! Matthew 23:27, "Woe to you, hypocrite scribes and Pharisees, because you are like graves that have been whitewashed, which on the outside are indeed shining beautiful, but on the inside they are filled with dead bones and everything unclean." This again was meant to be a wakeup call, a cold bucket of water in the face to shake the blinders off of their spiritual eyes. Y'shua wasn't just trying to be "mean" and make Himself look good at their expense. This was a righteous anger fueled by a passion for truth, and an overwhelming love that wants to save them and all who heard Him before it was too late. Christ was declaring that not only were they in gross error about His Word, but they going to hell and they were taking a lot of His children with them.

Spirit led rebuke is always done with the undertone of love and the desire to see reconciliation. Even if it seems harsh and overwhelming on its face, the end result is to bring about change which leads to salvation. Again, if the Lord was truly a God of unbridled wrath and fury, then why would He go out of His way to warn sinners of what was to come? We saw it with Moses warning Pharaoh in Egypt, the countless times He warned Israel in the wilderness, when he sent angels to warn Lot of the coming doom of Sodom and Gomorrah, and all of the major and minor prophets that followed. Moreover, Christ said that He can do nothing but the will of His Father, so the desires of His heart towards us has not changed. Speaking the truth in love does not mean we sacrifice passion or boldness.

What should concern us more? The thought of someone not liking us, or the thought of someone spending an eternity separated from God? Christ fully comprehended the hell that awaited the scribes, Pharisees, and a large portion of Israel at the time. He should; He was the One Who created it for Satan and his demons, not us. If you read this passage of scripture as a crying out to repentance, the ferocity in which Christ spoke makes so much more sense. Again, if He truly hated us, then all He would have to do is nothing and we would suffer for all of eternity. However, if He loves us beyond what we could possibly comprehend, then He would spend our every waking moment pursuing us and drawing us back to Himself.

I remember reading a news article years ago about a ten year old boy who was attacked by an alligator in Florida. The boy had begged his father to let him go swimming in their pool in the back yard, and the father finally agreed to let him. As the young boy sprinted to the pool, the father saw what looked like a large log floating in the water. By the time the father had realized it was an alligator, his son had already jumped in. As the father ran and screamed frantically for his son to get out, the gator had already started moving in for the kill. Just as the father jerked his son out of the water, the alligator clamped its jaws down on the boy's legs and they were caught in a deadly tug of war match. After what seemed like an eternity, the father was able to pull his son free, but the act of pulling his son away caused the alligator's teeth to do extensive damage to the boy's legs. A week or so after the attack, a news reporter came to interview the boy and see how he was doing. Not wanting to traumatize the child again, the reports asked if he could see the boy's "really cool scars." The boy showed the reporter his legs, and the reporter praised him on how great they looked. The boy then told the reporter "that's nothing, look at my arms!"

As the reporter look at the boy's arms, he noticed similar scaring and he asked if the alligator had bitten him there as well. Boy said, "Nope, that's how much my daddy loves me." The scars on the boy's arms were from his father's fingernails as he was trying to pull his son to safety. In Proverbs 27:6 the Lord tells us that "Faithful are the wounds of a friend, but the kisses of an enemy are abundant." We have to rid ourselves of the "New Age" mindset that there is no love in rebuke or correction. To tolerate the sins of another is to assist them in their journey to hell. The Lord adamantly corrected those who He loved, in hopes of bringing them to a place where they could spend an eternity with Him. And as we have seen so many times before, there is no shadow of change in Him.

Be ever watchful:

Proverbs 25:2 says, "It is the honor of God to conceal a thing, but the honor of kings is to search out a matter." There are certain things that the Lord will reveal to us, and then there are answers He wants us to dig for. As I said before, often times Christ would give His listeners all the information they needed to get a revelation, without telling it to them out right. This would allow them to experience that "ah ha" moment that would stick in their memory. This teaching method continues here as Y'shua is telling His followers what to look for when waiting for His second coming. Again, we have a beautiful example of love in the form of a warning. In chapter 24 of Matthew, the disciples are asking what to look for when Christ returns and the Lord gives them tremendous insight.

First, He warns them about the false prophets and teachers coming in His name and that many would be deceived. I imagine that this would not have been too difficult for them to grasp, seeing how so many of their fellow Jews had fallen into Greek Mythology and the Babylonian Mysteries of the Romans. If you remember, Nimrod and Samuramous declared themselves to be gods and thus was the beginning of the "Mysteries" belief system. Christ continues by telling His disciples about famines, earthquakes, wars and rumors of war, and the persecution of the those who believe. What is particularly interesting in this warning is in verse 12 which reads "...and because of the increase of lawlessness the love of many will grow cold." We can already see evidence of this all around us today, and every one of these ear marks of Christ' coming continue to become more commonplace. However, we are seeing these things now and this warning was written down approximately fifty years after Y'shau's death.

So who is this love-motivated warning and stern call to be watchful written to? Us! The Lord was giving them insight into what was coming even though they were not going to be alive to see it. So this warning was meant to be generational, that each new son or daughter was to be looking intently for these things. The Lord did the same for Abraham about what was going to happen to his descendants in Egypt. Genesis 13:16 reads, "And He said to Abram, 'Know of a surety that your seed will be a stranger in a land that is not theirs and will serve them and they will afflict them four hundred years. And also that I AM will judge that nation whom they will serve, and afterwards they will come out with great possession. And you will go to your fathers in peace: you will be buried in a good old age. But in the fourth generation they will return here again, for the iniquity of the Amorite is not yet full."

The Lord of course fulfilled this warning and promise to the letter in that Abraham had Isaac, Isaac had Jacob who became Israel, and Jacob had Joseph who would later bring Israel into Egypt. The love of many growing cold will be due to the fact that they did not receive or believe this loving warning. For many, they will be blindsided and will question how such a loving God could allow this to happen. The Lord even takes His graciousness a step further when He promises to shorten the days because of His "elect" (verse 22). The Lord is not only giving a glimpse of what is coming, but how to prepare for it as well.

Now, I know the moment you read that your brain went to Matthew 24:36 which reads, "But no man knows about that Day and hour, and neither do the angels of the heavens nor the Son, except the Father only." You are right to have this be your first response, and I am by no means attempting to predict the exact day of His coming. However, I do believe the Lord is giving us an idea of the season of His coming. My reasoning for this is twofold which are in verses 31-33 that says, "Then He will send His angels with a great shofar call, and they will gather His chosen ones from out of the four winds as far as the uttermost parts of the heavens. But you learned the parable from the fig tree: now when its branch would become tender and it would put forth its leaves, you know that summer is near: so then you, when you would see all these things, you know that He is near the doors." First is the blowing of the shofar to gather His chosen to him, and this is where the commandments of the Lord come into play. In Leviticus 23, we see these commandments in a chapter that is often referred to a "God's Calendar." The two feast that hold significance in this case would be the Day of Memorial (or Yom Teru'ah) and the Day of Atonement (Yom Kippur). Yom Teruah is also known as the "Feast of Trumpets" which was followed by ten days afterwards with Yom Kippur. Yom Teruah is now more commonly known today as Rosh HaShanah or "head of the year." It was changed to Rosh HaShanah in 70 AD after the destruction of the second temple; however, it is also believed the this decision was influenced while Israel was in exile in Babylon to coordinate with their pagan new year. (8) This may seem trivial, but the change is quiet drastic and it makes sense why the enemy would want to mask the meaning. Teruah also means "shouting" or raising a noise, and there is no real reason in the Torah why this day is celebrated except to rest and offer sacrifices.

    This feast is very unique, because it is the only one that begins on a New Moon. Since they did not have telescopes during that time, they would have to go out every night and look to the heavens to find it. During this feast, a shofar would be sounded one hundred times that served as a calling to repentance. There are four primary types of shofar blasts: Tekiah – A long single blast (the sound of the King's coronation), Shevarim – Three short wail-like blasts (signifying repentance), Teru'ah – Nine staccato blasts of alarm (to awaken the soul), and Tekiah ha Gadol – A great long blast (for as long as you can hold it). (8)

During the ten days between, there was a plea for the people to repent and return to the Lord. When Yom Kippur came, it was the day when judgement was cast or a closing of the book. The symbolism here is nothing short of incredible. You have a mysterious feast that seems to have no purpose when it was commanded, they would have to watch the heavens closely to know when it began, they would blow shofars to call people to repentance with a sense of urgency, for they knew that judgement was coming soon. The Jews have been practicing the rapture since Leviticus! Now, I am not saying that Yom Kippur is the official day of Christ's return. His Word is very clear on that point; however, I do believe that if we continue to pursue Him in His Word, then we will be able to recognize the signs of His return as clearly as the olive leaves. Not to mention, what better way to build an excitement and expectation of His return then to practice celebrating it. If this wasn't enough, we are to celebrate it as a group of believers per God's command. In Leviticus 23:24 the Lord declares that this feast is to be a "holy convocation." The word "convocation" literally means a large formal assembly of people (9); so this is to be a reverent dress rehearsal of His coming! For so many years, the church has taught the return of Christ as something to fear with the whole Hell, fire, and brimstone approach. Though there is some truth to that teaching, we cannot stay stuck on that extreme. Yes, there will be a punishment for sin and those who reject the Lord. Yes, there will be weeping and gnashing of teeth in place where the fire and torment can never be quenched; that is not how the Lord wants the story to end. Just look at all of the effort He has gone through to tell us of His coming. This is not the wrath filled words of a Supernatural dictator ready to rule with an iron hand. This is the plea of the lover of our souls. A call to keep an eye to the heavens and our hands to the plow; so when He returns, He will find His bride ready to receive Him and spend an eternity by His side.

So why all of the talk about Hell, war, famine, pestilence, and the love of many growing cold? Simple: the Lord's heart and His character has not changed since the beginning. He loves us, and He wants us to know what He is planning to do so we will be prepared. Modern day weddings include engagement notifications, RSVP's, wedding dates, times, and locations. The bride and groom go above and beyond to make sure that everyone they love knows when the wedding will be. Plus, they make sure that everyone knows well in advance so preparations can be made by those attending. It is estimated that the Book of Leviticus was written in 1440 B.C., which means that the Lord commanded His people to begin practicing Yom Teruah (Feast of Trumpets) almost 3500 years ago. I think it is safe to say: the Lord has given us ample time to prepare for the greatest wedding in all of created history. He doesn't want us to miss it! So when a Christian makes the comment that the return of Christ is "scary," remind him or her it is love that is coming for them.

Chapter 10

Greater love hath no one...

      Our journey through the Word has finally brought us to this moment. Due to the fact that Matthew's account is very detailed, and the gospels cover very similar accounts of the life Christ, there is no need to go through them as we did the Torah. Though I do strongly encourage you to read though the gospels, seeing how each writer gives a unique perspective as to what Christ did in His ministry. For us, we now stand at the foot of a very familiar sight: the cross. Endless teaching and sermons have covered this critical point in history as the moment we were delivered from the wages of our sin, when the door to Heaven was finally opened to us that we may spend an eternity with him. However, by casting aside the Hebraic roots of what Christ did, when it happened, and why it occurred the way it did, it leaves us lacking so much in our understanding. This is where everything that was done and written since Genesis comes together. Not one word was without purpose, not one action without a plan. As I have said time and again, the Lord was setting the stage for His Son and this is the climactic scene to this carefully written script. Instead of simply reading the account of Y'shua's death and resurrection, let's take a cue from all of the times He was referred to as the "sacrificial lamb," and view this entire event through the eyes of Passover.

Looking for Blemishes:

If you haven't picked up on the pattern of the Word yet; to get the revelation, you have to go backwards before you can go forward. We pick up with Christ and His disciples on the Mount of Olives. We will come back to the Seder meal and other events leading up to this point later on; trust me, it will be worth the wait. Christ and His disciples are on the Mount of Olives, and the Lord has asked them to pray as He goes on a little further. This is another example about how location means so much, and can be easily over looked. In an article by Joseph Prince, *"Understanding the Significance of the Olive Tree and Anointing Oil,"* we see why Y'shua chose this place to pray and seek the Lord. In the article, Joseph recalls his trip in Israel and the three uses of the oil. "The guide explained that olive berries were put in the press and crushed with a huge millstone. The first press produces extra virgin olive oil, which is used to light the Jewish temple. The oil from the second press is used for medicine, while the oil from the third or last press is used for making soap." Y'shua went to the Mount of Olives to begin the process of becoming our Healing Oil! He was pressed by the enemy to the point of sweating blood so that He might become the Light of our salvation, our healing, and to cleanse us from all unrighteousness.

Now that the oil has been prepared, it is time for it to be harvested. Judas and the Temple guards find Christ and arrest Him after He is betrayed with a kiss, a mocking act of love interestingly enough. However, His love was demonstrated from the moment they seized Him, not only by healing the servant's ear after Peter cut it off, but also by preparing Peter for his upcoming failure. If you remember, Simon tells Christ that he will never abandon Him and Y'shua's response remains true to His character. In Luke 22:31 we read, "Simon, Simon! Behold Satan demanded to sift you all like wheat: but I have asked concerning you that your faith would not fail: and you, when you have returned must at once strengthen your brothers." Just like we saw in the previous chapter, and just like what we saw with Abraham, Christ loved Peter enough to warn him of what was coming. Yet, He didn't stop there. The Lord not only anticipated Peter's fall, He looked past it before it even occurred and gave Peter a mission when he "returned" or repented. This is the kind of God we serve that has already looked past our failures, and He still has a plan and a purpose for us. I have heard it asked if the Lord forgives future sins, to which I respond: when Christ died for us, all of our sins were future sins. This revelation of God's love was just too good to pass up!

As we continue our journey to the cross, we see Y'shua begin to take on the image of a sin offering. In Luke

22:63-65 we read, "And the men holding Him were mocking and beating Him, then after they blindfolded Him they were asking Him saying, 'You must prophesy now, who is the one who hit you?' And they were saying many other blasphemous things to Him." On the surface, this may seem like the temple guards were simply being cruel to Y'shua and I am sure that was their intentions. However, I submit to you an incredible act of love happening even now. Leviticus 4 describes the process the priest would go through for a sin offering which is what Christ is. In verse 33 we read, "And he (the priest) will lay his hand on the head of the sin offering and slay it for a sin offering in the place where they killed the burnt offering." It was the belief that by laying hands upon the head of the sacrifice, sin would be transferred onto the animal. Here is Christ being led to a place where burnt offerings were killed, and having hands laid upon His head in the form of fist. What a thought that Christ could have been taking upon Himself the sins of His abusers every time they hit Him! After all we have read leading to this point, would we expect anything less from such a loving and merciful God?

    Y'shua is then led before the Sanhedrin where they would seek to find a charge against Him. It has been taught that while they were questioning Christ, the lamb who had been selected by the high priest for the Passover sacrifice would have been getting examined for blemishes. At the same time, these two event would have been paralleling each other. In his book *"The Seven Feasts of the Messiah,"* Eddie Chumney wrote "The lamb that was to be slain by the high priest was led into the temple (Beit HaMikdash) and put in a prominent place of display. Likewise, Yeshua the Lamb of G-d went on public display when He entered the temple (Beit HaMikdash) and spent four days there among the people, the Sadducees, the Pharisees, and the scribes, as the leaders asked Yeshua their hardest questions. Yeshua was questioned in front of the people for four days, showing Himself to be without spot or blemish, fulfilling Exodus (Shemot) 12:5." Can you imagine the patience and the restraint it took Y'shua to sit and be questioned on the Word that He not only wrote, but Who He was? Christ was then led to Pilate, then Herod, and back to Pilate and neither man could find a reason to kill Him. Pilate even offered a choice to the people as to whether they wanted Y'shua or Barabbus, and they chose Barabbus. In Matthew 27:22-24 we read, "Pilate said to them, 'Then what should I do with Y'shua, the One called Messiah?' All said, 'He must be crucified!' But he said, 'For what evil did he do? And they were crying out even more saying, 'He must be crucified!' And when Pilate saw that it was not benefiting, but was becoming more turmoil, having taken water he washed his hands in the sight of the crowd saying, 'I am innocent from this blood: you see to it."

    I find it very interesting that in the four gospels, Matthew is the only one who took notice of Pilate washing his hands of Christ. This may seem metaphorical on the surface, but again, Y'shua is attempting to proclaim Himself to a Jewish people in a way they would understand. When the High Priest was finished examining the Passover lamb for blemishes or faults, he would signal those around him that the lamb was ready for sacrifice by washing his hands! The Jews at this time must have been so blinded by hate and tradition to not see the picture Christ was painting here. Pilate declared to them time and again that the Passover Lamb that a high priest (John the Immerser) had chosen, was without fault or blemish. The exact requirement necessary for their (and our) sins to be forgiven. Another incredible insight into this moment is the level of utter betrayal Christ experienced from His own, and the fact that John (Whom He loved) was the only one to document it.

    This would make sense seeing the love that John had for Christ, he would be able to pick up on the wounds of Y'shua's heart. In John 19:15 we read, "Then they cried out, 'You must take Him away! You must Him away! You must now crucify Him.' Pilate said to them, 'Will I crucify your King?' The high priest answered, 'We have no king except Caesar." At the time of Julius Caesar, most of the Roman empire were followers of the Babylonian Mysteries. Since the fall of Babylon, no one had filled the position of god and high priest of the Mysteries, giving Julius the opportunity to reach the level of deity in his follower's eyes. (11) Ever since then, the title of "Caesar" wasn't just one of political power, but that the person bearing the title was god. So when the Jewish leaders made the statement in front of Christ of "We have no king but Caesar," they were declaring "we choose the god of the Mysteries over you." God's chosen people were literally declaring their allegiance to the demonic over their Sin Offering that stood before them. This was the perfect reenactment of what took place at the base of Mount Sinai, when the children of Israel declared that the golden calf (a symbol of the Mysteries) had delivered them from Egypt. This gives a whole new meaning to the scripture in Romans 5:8, "....but God demonstrated His love for us Himself, because, although we were still sinners, Messiah died on our behalf."

Just Believe:

As Christ is being led to the place where He would give up His life, we see the image of Abraham and Isaac begins to emerge. If you remember the account in Genesis 22, Isaac is required to carry the wood of his own sacrifice up Mount Moriah. Plus, seeing Isaac was believed to be approximately 30 years old during this time, he could have easily overpowered his much older farther. This makes his actions even more Christ like in that he was a willing sacrifice who trusted the leadership of his father. Not to mention, Mount Moriah (God is teacher) would later become Jerusalem and this mountain would be called Golgotha. Again, the Lord has set the stage to declare the glory of Christ to the world. Yet, as this divine and awe inspiring play unfolds, we see Y'shua bring in some very unlikely co-stars on Golgotha. Though the two thieves He hung in between seem to play a small role, there is a very clear message that the Lord is wanting to convey. In Luke 23:39-43 we read, "Then one of the evil ones who was hanging there was blaspheming Him saying, 'Are You not the Messiah? You must now save Yourself and us.' But the other said, rebuking him, 'Do you not yourself fear God, because you are in the same sentence? But we indeed justly, for what we did is worthy of what we are receiving: but this one did nothing improper.' Then he was saying, 'Y'shua, You must right away remember me when You would enter You Kingdom.' Then He said to Him, 'Truly I say to you, this very day you will be with Me in Paradise." First off, it should be no surprise that the enemy would use one of the thieves to try and sway Christ one more time. Especially while Y'shua is in a tremendous amount of pain and His flesh is screaming. I know this ploy of the enemy in my own life all too well, and I am sure you do also. Yet, it is the thief that receives salvation that reveals the Lord's heart.

  Christ didn't look at the thief that cried out and say, "I would love to help you, but when was the last time you went to church? When was the last time you tithed? What denomination are you? Have you been baptized?" I know I am knocking over a lot of sacred cows here, but look at the message Y'shua is trying to convey in this simple act of love. He is declaring to us, and all who were watching, what the true road to salvation looks like. Consider what Paul wrote in Romans 10:9, "Because if you would confess with your mouth the Lord Y'shua and you would believe in your heart that God raised Him from the dead, you will be saved." Paul, who considered himself a Jew among Jews, who knew the Old Testament better than any of us ever could, makes this incredible profound and yet simple declaration of how to be saved. Just to clarify, I am by no means attempting to dismiss or minimize the topics of my previous example. All of these things, with the exception of denominations of course, are very important to our spiritual growth and wellbeing. However, we cannot allow for the "acts of righteousness" to replace the sincerity of our confession of faith, or the intimacy we so desperately need to have with Christ. It is our hearts that He is after, plain and simple. There is also a foreshadowing taking place here that the Lord wanted us to see as well. Luke notes in 23:33 that Christ was hung between the two thieves; this was not done by accident. The right hand of God symbolizes power and salvation, while the left contains destruction and judgement. We see this in Matthew 25:31-46 where He describes how He will judge the multitudes when He returns. The sheep will be placed on His right hand and the goats on His left hand. Which side of Christ do you think the thief that cried out hung on? Even during His death, He was proclaiming His return and salvation.

A Cry from the Cross:

      We can clearly see the perfection of our God on display so far. However, we have come to a place where the teaching about the crucifixion seems to get a little twisted. Now, I do not believe that this is being done by pastors/teachers intentionally to mislead or deceive. However, I can see how the enemy can benefit from this misrepresentation. About the ninth hour while Christ is nailed to the cross, He makes the statement "Eli, Eli, L'mah sh'vaktani?"Or in English, "My God! My God! Why have you utterly forsaken Me? (Matthew 27:45-46) I love asking fellow believers what they have been taught as far as why the Christ made this statement. Many provide me with the same answer, "Because the Lord turned His back on Him." I find that this teaching can be used as a ploy of the enemy in the belief that, if God turned His back on Christ, what chance do I have when I sin? The Lord has declared to us in Hebrews 13:5, "…I will never abandon you and I will not ever forsake you." This promise is repeated in Joshua 1:5 and in Deuteronomy 31:6, and our God does not have a shadow of change in Him. So why did He make the statement of being forsaken? The answer screams His heart towards us unlike any of the other times before.

      As I have mentioned before, in order for someone to become a Rabbi, they would need to have the entire Old Testament completely contributed to memory. Since they had this kind of knowledge of the Word, they could have Bible studies (if you will) without the need of scrolls. They would simply quote a portion of one of the writings and the other Rabbi would know where they were talking about. This was also done since they did not have chapters and verse back then the way we do now. For example, If you and I were having an "Old Testament style" Bible study and I said, "For I know the plans that I have for you, says the Lord, plans to prosper you and not to harm you. Plans to give you hope and an expected end." You would know that I was quoting from Jeremiah 29:11 and we would go from there with our study. Who was in attendance at Christ' crucifixion and was mocking Him? The Pharisees, Sadducees, and other religious leaders familiar with the Word. Y'shua wasn't just a Jewish carpenter; He was also a well-known and well respected Rabbi. So, what better way to try and reach those who were killing Him then to have one last Bible study. Remember, they would quote the first part of a passage so that the listener would know where in the Torah, Haf-Torah, and major/minor prophets the speaker was referring to.

In Psalms 22, the passage starts off with "My God, My God, why have You utterly forsaken Me?" If you continue to read, you find the passages in verses 15-19 "I am poured out like water and all My bones are out of joint. My heart is like wax, it is melted in the midst of My insides. My strength is dried up like a potsherd and My tongue cleaves to My jaws and You have brought Me into the dust of death, for dogs have surrounded Me, the assembly of the wicked has enclosed Me. Like a lion the tear My hands and My feet. I may tell all My bones: they look and stare upon Me. They part My garments among them and cast lots for My clothing." The 22nd Psalms is King David's perfect, prophetic account of the crucifixion. Even in verse 8-9, David says exactly what the religious leaders would say about Christ while he hung on the cross!

    When Christ's crying out is normally taught, one is left with the impression that He was out of control and completely helpless. He was at the mercy of the sickness, disease, and sin of the world that had been laid upon Him. No one could bear the wrath of God but God Himself. While Y'shua was suffering and dying, He wasn't questioning the One Who lead Him there. Christ knew exactly what was coming in the garden and why it had to be done. Y'shua was crying out in one last attempt to minster to the ones who were killing him! He was trying to get their minds back to Psalms 22 so they would fully understand what they were looking at. Christ did not want them to miss this moment, one that He had been preparing them for since Deuteronomy. This is not a scene of Christ reaching a point that was beyond His ability; this is the same being that spoke the worlds into existence. He measures the universe by the span of His hand, and He was in full power and control as He hung on the cross. He loved us so much that He was willing to die in our place, satisfying the wages of our sin. Moreover, He loved the ones screaming for His death so much that He tried to evangelize them one more time from the cross. There can be no greater example of His love for us than this selfless act, or of how far He is willing to go to capture our hearts.

One of the greatest deceptions of the enemy is the belief that we have strayed too far to be saved. We feel we are either out of God's reach, or we have become so dirty that He simply has no use for us now. It is almost as if we believe God didn't see our "kind of sin" coming when He died. I have even heard it asked if God is willing to forgive future sin; He died for us over almost 2000 years ago: all of our sin is future sin. When the Bible says that He bore all of our sins, it means ALL. By allowing the enemy to make us question this is to question God's power, His strength, His ability, and His relentless desire to be with us. Our biggest challenge most of the time is allowing ourselves to receive that love. More often than not, we feel unworthy of His love and we are. We feel like there is nothing we can do to earn His love and we are correct. However, this fact is not one that should create discouragement or hopelessness, but overwhelming joy and comfort. We do not deserve His love, yet He loves us anyway. There is nothing we can do to earn His grace, yet He calls us righteous. It was His love for us in spite of us, that drew our hearts to repentance in the first place. His cry from the cross proves that until we breathe our last breath, He will never stop warring for our hearts. I have heard it said that we can reject God, but He is going to make it very difficult to not fall in love with Him.

To reinforce the fact that the Lord was in complete control, we look at the final words He spoke on the cross. We see these immortal words in John 19:30, "Then when He took the sour wine Y'shua said, 'It has been completed,' and having bowed His head He gave up His spirit." The more common translation that people are familiar with is from the Latin, which says, "It is finished." When the final Passover sacrifice was completed, normally at 3 p.m., the priest would go to the highest point of the temple and blow a shofar. This was to declare to all in Jerusalem that their sins had been covered (not cleansed) for that year. If we go back to Exodus 19:16-20, we find that the blowing of the shofar was associated with the voice of the Lord.

The scriptures read, "And it was on the third day in the morning that there were thunders and lightnings and a thick cloud upon the mountain, and the sound of the shofar was exceedingly loud, so that all the people in the camp trembled. And Moses brought the people out of the camp to meet with God and they stood at the base of the mountain. And Mount Sinai was altogether in smoke, because the Lord descended upon it in the fire and its smoke ascended like the smoke of a furnace, and the whole mountain quaked greatly. And when the sound of the shofar sounded long and grew louder and louder, Moses spoke and God answered him audibly. And the Lord came down upon Mount Sinai, on the top of the mountain and the Lord called Moses up to the top of the mountain, and Moses went up." Where Christ was hanging on the cross, it would have been close enough for Him to hear the sounding of the shofar. I believe that what Y'shua was echoing what He heard the Father declaring from the top of the Temple, that His Son had paid the ultimate price in full and that "it is finished." The dividing wall between God and man had been forever removed. Even the veil was torn to show that He wanted nothing to separate us from Him, and all could experience His presence.

Love from the grave:

If Y'shua would have only died and went to Heaven, what hope would we have for our own salvation? Sure, He rose Lazarus from the grave while He was on the earth, but could we believe that power continued if He stayed dead? Y'shua had one more declaration of His love for us before leaving earth, one that would solidify the faith of His followers. He needed to show that He had power even over death, hell, and the grave. He had led captivity captive, and set the captives free. He went into the enemy's own territory, and stripped him once and for all of his power over us. Finally, His followers knew the heart of their Messiah and if He would do it for Himself, He would do it for them. I love the account in Luke 24:13-35 where two of the disciples were walking to Emmaus, and the Lord joins them cloaked as a stranger. He asked them what they were talking about and they were grieved to recount the death of their Savior. What I find so amazing about this passage is the fact that Y'shua didn't just simply reveal Himself to them. Instead, He took them back to the Old Testament to remind them of who He was and what He had to do. Verse 27 we read, "And beginning with Moses, and all the Prophets He explained to them with all the writings concerning Himself." He didn't remind them of all of the miracles He performed or the powerful messages He taught. Instead, He took them back to the "tutor" so they could fully understand what He did and why He did it. Then, I believe because He couldn't contain the joy of them knowing, Y'shua did something they have seen Him do before (break bread) and their eyes were opened. It wasn't enough that these two disciples knew it was Christ they were talking to. The Lord wanted them to be able to answer the questions others would have about Him. Not only what He did for them, but why He did it.

If you continue in this chapter, you find that Christ then revealed Himself to His disciples. This is so interesting because He didn't do it when they were out in public so all could fall and worship Him. He went to where they were hiding and met with them in a very intimate and personal way. He didn't demand that they believe, and then rebuke them for not putting faith in the fact that He told them He would rise again. Instead, He invites them to touch Him, to place their fingers in the holes in His hands and feet. He even goes so far as to eat in front of them to help them overcome their unbelief. Yet, then He does something that I mentioned in the very beginning of this book: He gave them a gift that we are entitled to, and it gave them a complete picture of His love for them. Luke 24:45-48 reads, "Then He opened their minds and they understood the Scriptures: and He said to them that "Thus it has been written that the Messiah would suffer and be raised from the dead on the third day, and repentance would be preached in His name for forgiveness of sins for all the heathens. Beginning from Jerusalem you are witnesses of these things." He opened their minds to scripture; I cannot even begin to imagine what that must have been like for them. Everything they have ever read or have been taught, from Genesis to Malachi, suddenly was inundated with purpose and revelation. For the first time in history, they were given the privilege of not only knowing the "what, where, and when" of God's word, but the "why." The feasts, the sacrifices, the Tabernacle, the Tzitzits, the Ark of the Covenant, they could finally see that it was all Y'shua from the very beginning. They now had a role in the play the Lord had been scripting since the Garden of Eden; when the power of the Holy Spirit came upon them, they began writing the script for our parts as well.

    It is absolutely imperative that we do not allow traditions, denominations, false religion, or theologies to close our minds to scripture. The Lord wants us to have a deep, working, and living knowledge of His love for us, not only so we can share that love with others, but so we can strengthen our own foundation against the attacks of the enemy. What can Satan do to a heart that is overflowing with love and confidence in that love? For too long, we have been told that aspects of the Word have been done away with, and it has been replaced with a very anti-sematic approach to scripture. Powerful accounts of God's perfect timing, unfailing love, and unwavering grace have been replaced with either condemnation, or the dumbing down to a self-help book full happy thoughts and "positive energy." Hebrews 12:2 declares that Y'shua is the "Author and Finisher of the Faith," He knows exactly what our hearts need to remain firm in Him. That is why He went to such great lengths to set the stage for His coming, His ministry, and His second coming. Our eyes have been opened to scripture just as it was with the disciples. In Joel 3, the Lord said that He would pour out His spirit upon all flesh, and with that spirit comes understanding and revelation. The enemy has tried desperately to hide the love of our God from us, but there is a stirring that is causing us to seek His heart and not just His hand. All we have to do is continue to pursue Him with His complete and unfailing Word that will never pass away. Allow yourself to be captured by a God who has sought your heart since He formed it in your mother's womb. He has so much in store if we would only pursue Him the way He has pursued us.

One Last Glimpse:

     For years, I have wondered why the Lord continued to refer to His return as a wedding. Throughout scriptures, He uses wedding analogies to refer to Himself and the church, and I always assumed it was because weddings are a joyous occasion full of love. If you remember when Jacob wrestled with the "Man," we found that the Hebrew word for "man" in this passage is "Ish," meaning "Bridegroom." This reference to a bridegroom clearly showed us that the "Man" Jacob wrestled was Christ. It wasn't until I learned of the Hebrew wedding process that I saw just how the Lord was pulling everything together. In order for the process to begin, the groom would go to the bride's father to ask for her hand in marriage. Since that groom would be removing a source of income for the bride's family, there was a price to be paid (or Mohar) and a contract was signed known as a "Katubah." Not only would this help compensate the family, but it would also demonstrate the love the groom had for the bride. If I would have gone to my now father-in-law and had we used this process, what do you think he would have done to me if I offered him $20 for his daughter? Even a non-Jewish person could quickly see the lack of commitment and love in my offer; knowing my father-in-law, him saying "no" would have been the least of my concerns. The amount of love is demonstrated by the price willing to be paid. Romans 8:32 says, "He in fact did not spare His own Son but gave Him over on behalf of us all, then how will He not freely give us all things with Him?" What price was our Groom willing to pay for us? Everything. Interestingly enough, when the Ketubah was signed, the bridegroom would declare in a loud voice "It is finished" or "paid in full."

    Next, the groom would then leave to prepare a place for his bride or a "Chuppah" (12). This new home would be an addition to the groom's father's home which was begun by the father. Even in Israel today, you can see homes that have a door leading to a graded piece of land. When you see this, you know that a son lives there and they have already prepared a place for the son to build his home. In John 14:2-4 we read "In My Father's house there are many dwelling places: and if it were not so, would I tell you that I am going to prepare a place for you? And if I would go, then I shall prepare a place for you. I am coming again and I shall take you along with Me, so that where I AM you would also be. And you know the way, where I am going." The groom would leave gifts for the bride to be reminders of him during this time of separation. We can find our gifts in 1 Corinthians 12:8-11, "For indeed through the Spirit to one is given a word of wisdom, and to another a word of knowledge according to the same Spirit, to another faith by the same Spirit, and to another gifts of healing by the one Spirit, and to another activities that call forth miracles, and to another prophecy, and to another discerning spirits, to another to speak in different kinds of tongues, and to another interpretation of tongues, but the one Spirit operates all these things, distributing His own gifts to each, just as He wishes." Notice that the word "gift" is used several times in this passage. These gifts were never meant to create division, cults, or denominations that wanted nothing to do with each other. They were purely intended to edify the church, to be reminders of our Groom, and to prepare us for His return. Isn't it amazing how the enemy has so twisted the purpose of these precious gifts, that many Christians want nothing to do with them? Not only does this create confusion in the body of Christ, but it greatly hinders our effectiveness to further the Kingdom of God. And at the risk of sounding redundant, they are gifts! Not earned nor deserved, but gifts of love to be reminders of the One Who is coming for us. Take the spiritual prayer language or "speaking in tongues" as it is commonly referred to. This incredible, tangible example of the presence of our God has been so abused, that the church often goes to two extremes on it. One camp will say that if you do not possess this gift, then the Holy Spirit does not dwell within you, therefore you are not saved. The other camp says that this gift has been fulfilled and no longer exists. We know that the enemy is the author of confusion; and we also know that when we don't understand something about the word or it makes us uncomfortable, then we simply dismiss it as "not for us." The truth is that neither are correct. What could be more intimate than to have your own personal prayer language, given to you by someone who adores you, so you could speak to your King in a way that even the enemy cannot understand?

Notice what the end of that passage in 1 Corinthians 12:11 says about these wedding gifts. "...the one and the same Spirit operates all these things, distributing His own gifts to each, just as He wishes." I have even been in a church where a young woman had gone up to the alter and had genuinely given her life to Christ. The following couple of weeks, she broke up with her boyfriend whom she was in sin with, she quit ALL of the drugs and alcohol she had been abusing, and was excited to learn about her new life in Christ. Talk about bearing fruit worthy of repentance! However, there was a problem with her walk according to this church. For the next two Sundays following her salvation, she had gone up to the alter to "receive the Holy Ghost," but she was not getting her "baptism in the spirit." For this church, the only true manifestation of the Holy Spirit filling someone is for them to start speaking in tongues. When she asked why she wasn't receiving the gift, the church leaders told her that they didn't know. When she asked them if she were to die would she go to heaven, they told her "no." This left this young lady confused and hurt, "I thought God loved me, why doesn't He want me to go to Heaven?" Can you see where the author of confusion comes in? Not only for the young lady, but also for this specific church whose entire theology was just turned on its head.

Which leads me to this question: if the Spirit of God had not filled this young lady the moment she committed her life to Christ, do you truly think she would have the spiritual strength or emotional courage to give up so much sin so quickly? She was able to do in a matter of weeks what it takes most people years to accomplish. The love of the world that dwelled within her had suddenly been replaced by true love, a gift from her new Bridegroom. This new perspective on the spiritual gifts completely did a number in my own heart, having been brought up in the Pentecostal church. Pursuing the gifts and the presence of the Holy Spirit is a great thing, but not at the expense of the One Who sent him.

Since the gifts and the uses of them have been twisted, many people have a tendency to place the Holy Spirit Himself on the back burner of their walk. Yet, the next step in the Hebrew wedding process shows that this is incredibly detrimental. When the groom would leave his fiancé to prepare a place for them to live, he would leave a servant or a trusted friend to help the bride to be ready for the big day of his return. In John 16:5-7 we see the trusted friend Christ left with us. "But now I am going to the One Who sent Me, and none of you can ask Me, 'Where are you going?' But, because I have spoken these things to you, sorrow has filled your hearts. But I am telling you the truth, it is profitable for you that I would leave. For if I would not leave, the Comforter will not come to you: but if I would go back, I will send Him to you." With this in mind, doesn't it make sense why the enemy would try to get us to distance ourselves from our Comforter? This powerful ally was sent for the sole purpose of preparing us for Christ's return. He woos us to repentance, He gives us the power to overcome the enemy, He gives us revelation, and makes us sensitive to the desires and movements of our King. He also gives us discernment with the hurts and needs of others so they too might be able to partake in the wedding. What a wonderful thought it is to know that our King didn't leave us to our own devices. He could have simply said, "I am leaving and you better be ready when I get back, or there will be Hell to pay." Then He takes off and we are left to guess what He wants us to do, or if it will even be enough for Him. Instead, He does the extreme opposite. He gives us a love letter declaring His heart, and a trusted friend to guide us right into His open arms.

    While the groom was preparing a place for his bride, neither one of them knew when the actual wedding day would be. That is due to the fact that it was the groom's father who would determine when the place was finished. This concept should ring a bell as far as what Y'shua said in Matthew 24:36, "But no one knows about that Day and hour, neither do the angels of the heavens nor the Son, except the Father only." What a breathtaking place Y'shua is making must be. He created all we have ever known in seven days, and here He has been working on a place for us for thousands of years! With all of His power and creative ability, He still waits for the Father to tell Him when it will be enough. We can always tell how much love someone has placed into a gift by the amount of time they spent preparing it. This place He is preparing for the ones He loves (us) is not being done carelessly. It is to be an eternal representation of just how much He loves us! When the groom's father finally said that the place was ready, the groom would go for his bride and it would often be at night. Again, does this sound familiar? "And concerning the times and the seasons, brothers, you do not need it to be written to you, for you know accurately that the Day of the Lord is coming like a thief at night." (1 Thessalonians 5:1-2) He would then go to the gate of his bride's house and blow a shofar, then the two would meet half way, and they would leave to prepare the wedding. (4) This is the story of the Rapture! The bride's responsibility was to make sure that her bags were packed, her dowry was ready, and that her lamp was filled with oil.

    This is where everything that we have read through from Genesis until now comes together. He desired a relationship with us and that relationship was broken. He then begins an incredibly patient and detailed process of restoring us to Himself. He sets the stage for His coming, gives us signs to look for, and feasts to practice so we would not miss Him. Because He loves us, Y'shua warned us about what was to come so we would not be caught off guard by our enemy. He became one of us so that we could know with assurance, that He knows exactly what we are going through no matter how hard. He suffers an unthinkable amount of pain to remove anything that would separate us from Him and His presence. Then, to summarize His heart towards us, He uses the ultimate ceremony of love to sum up His entire earthly ministry and His return. If all of this doesn't cause something in you to want to burst with joy and new found worth, then I don't know what will. To think, every time two of His chosen people took part in a traditional Hebrew wedding, they walk out Y'shua's heart. We cannot allow the god of this world to hijack this message and turn into a message of wrath or exclusion. His grace is abounding, His patience is without equal, and His love for us is without measure. The cry of my heart, and I believe that of the Lord's, as well, is that we worship and pursue Him in Spirit and complete truth. To not allow the schemes of the enemy or the theologies of men, which can often times be one in the same, to minimize or dismiss the heart of our God towards us. This is a love story that the world tries so desperately to replicate; however, our "happily ever after" has been paid in full and orchestrated since the foundation of the world.

References

Amaral, Joe. *Understanding Jesus*, New York NY: Faith Words, Hachette Book Group, 2011.

Morford, William J., *One New Man Bible, Revealing the Jewish Roots and Power,* True Potential Inc. 2011

www.templemount.org

Eldridge, John, *Wild at Heart.* Nelson Incorporated, Thomas 2001

Amplified Bible, Grand Rapids, Michigan, Zondervan 1987

Greenwood, Doug, *Follow Me, Reflections #908,* Preserving Bible Times, Blog 2008

Hebrew4christians.com

Random House Webster's College Dictionary, New York NY: Random House INC. 1997

Chumney, Eddie, *The Seven Festivals of the Messiah,* O Fallon Montana, Treasure House LLC, 1994

Fairley, Mark, *Know your enemy – Exploring the New World Order from a Christian Perspective,* DVD, The Fuel Project 2012

A Missing Link in Christianity, www.tasc-creationscience.org

Made in the USA
Las Vegas, NV
27 December 2021